"A fiercely honest and insightful read. I truly believe that
Dr. Sarah Coxon has written a book that should be in the
hands of every feminine being on this planet"
Africa Brooke, Mindset Coach, Speaker

"The Way of the Priestess is a raw and empowering initiation
for anyone on the path of reclamation. Boldly illuminating the
gaps in our approach to the Sacred Feminine and the wounds
so many women face, this book gives a simple and yet
revolutionary approach to live authentically and
unapologetically. Sarah's story changeS the narrative around
empowerment and healing. This book is a must read for
anyone hearing the call to reclaim their inner priestess and
come home to self."
Dr. Cassandra Wilder, Naturopathic Doctor and Founder of
'Goddess Ceremony'

"Sarah has truly shown me the way of the priestess. With her
authentic, no BS approach, she has helped me liberate and
empower myself as a spiritual female entrepreneur. When you
dive into these pages, know that you're in for a radical
homecoming to your most aligned and inspired self. Sarah's
work has been transformational in the way that I live my life
and I'm so excited for you to see the limitless possibilities
available to you as well."
Leneth Witte, Founder of 'The Spiritual Feminist'

"Reading this book feels like coming up for a gasp of fresh air
in a world where owning your true feminine power is still
discouraged. Through her account of historic priestesshood,
personal experience & coaching insights, Sarah gives you a
permission slip to become the person that, deep down, you
always knew you were. Sarah inspires, empowers & moves you
to unleash your magic and as such be a part of the rebalancing
needed in our world."
Isabelle Ysebaert, Msc. Psychologist & Coach and Founder of
'Full of Joy'.

THE WAY OF THE
PRIESTESS

THE WAY OF THE PRIESTESS

A RECLAMATION OF FEMININE POWER AND DIVINE PURPOSE

SARAH COXON, PHD

ISBN: 978-1-913590-11-6

The Unbound Press
www.theunboundpress.com

Hey unbound one!

Welcome to this magical book brought to you by The Unbound Press.

At The Unbound Press we believe that when women write freely from the fullest expression of who they are, it can't help but activate a feeling of deep connection and transformation in others. When we come together, we become more and we're changing the world, one book at a time!

This book has been carefully crafted by both the author and publisher with the intention of inspiring you to move ever more deeply into who you truly are.

We hope that this book helps you to connect with your Unbound Self and that you feel called to pass it on to others who want to live a more fully expressed life.

With much love,
Nicola Humber

Founder of The Unbound Press

www.theunboundpress.com

This book is dedicated to YOU. It's dedicated to all women who are dedicated to living a meaningful life.

To those of you who I've already had the honour to work with in my programmes and mentoring containers, thank you. Your hunger for this work and your willingness to dig deep and be beacons for reclamation has inspired me more than you know. To those of you who are new to my work, I'm incredibly grateful that you followed your curiosity and chose to dance with this book. I hope it inspires you to live a vibrant and fulfilled life.

To sisterhood and the reclamation of the feminine!

CONTENTS

PROLOGUE

I'm writing and birthing this book in the spring/summer of 2020. My Big Fat Portuguese wedding to my Italian love, Mauro, has been postponed because of the recent pandemic. The Black Lives Matter movement has been accelerated by the recent murders of Breanna Taylor and George Floyd. There have been fires raging around the globe. There's a bigger plan at work for this year. So, rather than organising wedding guests, I find myself channelling a book whose time has come. This is our work as priestesses — to respond and act as channels through which healing can flow.

This book is about reclaiming our feminine power, honouring our callings, and healing our planet. Essentially, it's a big 'fuck you' to the system. It's for you if you feel like you're here for more and you desire to live a life of purpose and liberation. It's for any woman who wants to come home to her authentic self, reclaim her feminine power, share her voice, own her gifts, and create a life of freedom. It's for the woman who wants to move beyond the toxic stories that she's been telling herself about not being good enough, experienced enough, or qualified enough to make a difference, and is ready to follow her callings and unapologetically step into her own unique priestesshood.

I have found that following our callings is a powerful way for women to reject and release themselves from circumstances that limit their feminine freedom, creative expression, and capacity to heal the planet. Stepping into priestesshood is about reclamation and creation. In my experience, when a woman reclaims her passions and gifts, and channels them into her purpose, she's able to create a life that frees her soul and ignites her spirit. This is why, as well as the deep inner work of feminine reclamation, I also share within these pages my entrepreneurial journey and how this has been a powerful vehicle for my healing and expansion. My intention is that it inspires you to follow the callings of your own inner priestess and create fulfilment and abundance on your terms.

The process of reclaiming the feminine is unique for each of us and yet there are universal themes that bring us together in our quest for liberation. We can only transform what we can see and so my intention within this book is to illuminate your personal path using the mirror of my own story as well as the stories of some of my clients. When we share our truth as women, it becomes medicine for the collective. I share with you the twists and turns of my own journey, from feeling unworthy and disconnected, to owning my priestesshood and thriving. I share with you how I've begun the lifelong process of transcending the limitations of my cultural conditioning to live my purpose. I tell my story of learning to share my voice, how I built a thriving impactful business, how I've embodied more abundance than ever before, and how I'm building a life that I don't need a vacation from. I also share practices that have helped me and my clients in our personal journeys of feminine reclamation and divine purpose.

As you read this book, it's important to remember that the ways in which you will channel your priestesshood will be unique to you. You may choose to create, or teach, or guide. Stay open to what's calling you as you read these pages and remember that, although your journey may mirror my story in many ways, your path is completely your own. Within this book, you'll find yourself reflected back to you through the mirror of my truth. And with this, you'll begin to understand the external and internalised systems of oppression that have held you back from being who you're meant to be, and the necessary shifts needed to move forward. This isn't a 'how to' book. This is a book about your own personal power. The power of the priestess. Once you activate this, anything is possible.

I don't have all the answers for you because I'm still learning, and to pretend anything else would be disempowering for you. We are all women in process, me included. There truly is no destination, no magical place that we can get to that will make us feel worthy and enough. There is only the journey. And rather than being a linear five-step plan, the wisdom in this book has come through as a feminine non-linear patchwork of stories and observations. It will serve as a mirror for your own contemplations and unfolding. Our personal growth isn't linear and there is no end point. Trying to live life as though it is is actually part of the issue. When we don't allow ourselves to always be in process, we continue to think that there's something wrong with us and that we must try harder to improve and 'get there'. I spent years of my life believing that I was flawed and that one day, when I finally got all my shit together and transcended all my blocks and conditioning, I'd feel amazing and that would be it — mission accomplished. My greatest liberation came when I understood that, as long as I'm breathing, I'm going to be in process, and the day I stop growing will be the day of my death. It's the same for all of us.

In many ways, despite having been on the journey of reclamation for over 15 years, I feel like I've only just begun this work. It's likely that as soon as this book goes to print, my understanding of feminine power and the priestess will have already changed. I ask you to simultaneously call out and forgive me for any blind spots that there may be in this book or any assumptions that have been made. I'm learning just like you.

Sweet relief comes when we radically accept where we are in our process. Creativity and inspiration come when we stop measuring ourselves up against where we think we should be. My biggest hope for you is that, as you read this book, you don't compare yourself to me and where I am on my journey, instead you see your own path in a different light and feel inspired to live a life that's truer and more authentic to you, your desires and values.

Life as a modern-day priestess is full of truth, mission, purpose, healing and growth. As has been the case for me, it also leads to abundance and a better sense of belonging in a world that can often feel like it's trying to tear us down. Being a priestess isn't about drinking turmeric lattes, burning sage, and doing yoga. It goes much deeper than that. It's about understanding the systems of oppression that affect how we show up in the world. It's about calling out institutions that marginalise people. It's about rejecting industries that destroy our earthly habitat. It's about learning how external oppression becomes internalised. It's about reclaiming our individual power and also reclaiming the feminine collectively. It's about honouring our gifts and living our purpose. It's about channelling this into ventures that make us feel fulfilled. And — and this is really radical — it's about creating a life that is full of joy.

It's no coincidence that you've picked up this book. What's written within these pages will be the catalyst for a completely new way of being and I'm excited for you. But now it's time to get to work. It's time to reclaim our feminine power and authentic selves. It's time to flow, create, express ourselves and be heard. It's time to live our dharma (divine mission). It's time to own our gifts. It's time to channel them into new projects and businesses that heal our planet. It's time to play bigger. It's time to create freedom on our own terms.

It's time to fully embody the magical being that you are and to become all you're meant to be.

INTRODUCTION

Many women in today's world feel a strong pull towards the priestess. Some may call it their inner witchiness or their inner 'woo' — but it's the same energy — an ancient remembering of feminine sovereignty. And in a world that continues to devalue the feminine, invoking the priestess is a route to the reclamation of individual and collective power and balance.

ICE CREAM

My dad has a story about me that he loves to tell to just about anyone who will listen. I was two years old and my mum, dad, older brother Nev and I were on a beach somewhere in France. Presumably, Nev was off making mischief somewhere and I was sat next to my parents, playing with the sand and minding my own business.

After some time I stood up, looked into the distance at an ice cream van that was parked on the other side of the beach, perhaps one kilometre away, and announced to my dad that it was time for ice cream. And when my dad gave me some BS reason as to why I couldn't have one, I glared at him defiantly, blonde curls dancing in the breeze.

'I'm going to get one,' I said, and despite having no money, my little two-year-old legs started carrying me in the direction of my chosen target.

My dad remembers laughing at me, watching me stomp across the sand, and waiting for me to get scared and come back. But I didn't. I kept marching on until my parents were mere dots in the distance. I didn't even look back at them.

By the time my dad had run to catch up with me, I was stood patiently in line at the van, waiting for my turn. Five minutes later, I'm walking back to my mum, holding my dad's hand, my face covered in ice cream and a satisfied grin.

This may sound like a story of childish defiance, greed, and maybe even privilege, but it's not. It's a story about a little girl who innocently followed her desires and knew her worth. It's a story of a little girl who went for what she wanted before the world told her why she shouldn't.

Because not long after the ice cream triumph, that little girl was conditioned to forget her autonomy and value. She learned to lock away her desires deep in the recesses of her inner world and to throw away the key for good measure. She learned that her purpose as a woman was simple: keep everyone happy, be a good girl, and most definitely never, ever have ideas about yourself that are above your station.

That two-year-old child grew into a young woman who didn't want to be seen as wanton or greedy. She did not dare to shine her light or ask for what she wanted. She did not dare rock the boat. She did not dare think she was worthy or capable of bigger things.

Consequently, during my early twenties, I found myself riddled with insecurity and bound by fear and social expectation. And in a world preoccupied with the material, I also felt cut off from the spiritual. Somewhere, in the depths of my core, I knew that I was here to experience more connection to my true self, share my voice and make a bigger impact.

Over the past decade, I've been on a journey of radical reclamation. The trajectory of my exploration has taken many strange and unusual turns but it eventually led me to discover the truest essence within me: the priestess. And in the wake of reconnecting to her, I found the bravery to leave behind the toxic web of inherited social expectations I found myself in and, instead, to reclaim my priestess powers and channel them into a vocation of my choosing.

This book is about that journey. It's both my personal memoir and a call to arms for any woman who feels trapped in a social cage that stifles her truest expression. It's for any woman brave enough to walk a new path, reclaim her power, walk hand in hand with the Divine, and live authentically, freely and purposefully.

I'm going to be taking you on a journey of your own reclamation, sharing stories to bring about recognition and illumination in your own life, as well as the tools that have helped me and my clients to come into the fullest expressions of ourselves as women and to live more expansively.

The stories I share in this book represent lessons I have learned in my life so far. Everything I have written is true, to my memory, but please bear in mind that there are two sides to every story. I have also changed the names of individuals in some instances in order to maintain their anonymity.

The codes written within these pages will activate your priestesshood. They will help you reclaim your authentic self, your gifts and your dharma. They will help you step out of the cage of your current existence and into a new way of being so that you can follow your callings and experience soul satisfaction.

This book is for the woman feeling the call to rise up, stand in her power and leave her legacy here on earth. It's for the woman who feels in her bones the call to say 'no' to systems that breed prejudice, discrimination, greed and injustice. It's for the woman who wants to create heaven here on earth. And it's for the woman who wants to transcend her inherited fear, reclaim her creative magic, find her voice and express herself unapologetically so that she can inspire and lead others to do the same.

IT'S ALL ANCIENT HISTORY

At nine years old my teacher asked me what I wanted to be.

'An archaeologist,' I proudly announced.

For as long as I could remember, the ancient world had been calling to me, beckoning me to pay her a visit and remember her. As a child, I wasn't able to fully comprehend or articulate why I wanted to be an archaeologist. But as I grew older, it became clearer. I felt like I didn't belong in the modern world; the past felt like home to me and I ached to go back there.

At the age of 18, I left home to follow this calling. I went down the only route I knew at the time — I enrolled in a university degree. Three years of undergraduate study gave way to a Masters degree and then a PhD. There was no stopping me. My ravenous hunger to understand my heritage was insatiable and I was privileged enough to be able to follow my curiosity.

I now recognise that I was never destined to 'be' an archaeologist — it was never my true dharma or identity. It was simply a breadcrumb and a piece of the puzzle.

What I learned during my time as an academic not only shaped my understanding of the modern world but also lit a fire inside me. During my first semester as an archaeology student, I learned why women globally have been treated as second-class citizens for millennia. And it pissed me off.

PATRIARCHY: A BRIEF HISTORY

I'm 19 years old and sat in the front row of the lecture theatre.

This was unusual — the front row was notoriously reserved for mature students. I wasn't mature (in any sense of the word) and yet I purposefully sat there, completely transfixed.

Yvonne was one of my favourite lecturers and the module she was teaching was Feminist Archaeology. A liberal herself, with short hair, tawny eyes, and long dangly earrings, it was Yvonne who introduced me to the work of feminist legends such as Simone de Beauvoir, Judith Butler, and Angela Davis. And it was during her lectures that my deepest suspicions were confirmed: patriarchy is the sea that we swim in and the air that we breathe and it underpins almost every facet of social structure. In fact, we've been living under the patriarchal shadow for over 3500 years.

Patriarchy is an ideology and system of oppression where power is held by men because men are seen as superior. It's extremely hierarchical in nature and the predominant themes of patriarchy are competition, dominance, aggression, force and control. Within the patriarchal paradigm, the feminine is devalued.

Seeing men as the default gender runs deep within the fabric of society. There's an imbalance in the representation of men and women everywhere: in history, film, books and the media. What is male is seen as universal whereas what is female is seen as niche. You only have to browse Netflix to recognise this — 'Strong Female Lead' should not be a category unless there's also the category of 'Strong Male Lead' which, of course, there isn't. In fact, my partner and I were recently given the bank cards for our first joint bank account. As we ripped open the envelope, we discovered that on his card he had been upgraded to 'Dr' even though he doesn't have a doctorate. This was of course an oversight on the bank's part, but it says it all. The message was clear: women aren't supposed to outrank men.

The pain and oppression you have felt as a woman is real. And it's not your fault. Patriarchy is deeply entrenched within the bones of our society and it's the basis for all of the inequality that is experienced in the Western modern world, not only by women, but also by other marginalised groups.

It's important for me to highlight that my personal experiences of misogyny and discrimination are not universal. This is because I'm a white woman. Black women, indigenous women and women of colour experience this oppression differently. I'm also heterosexual and cisgender. Those who identify as LGBTQ also experience oppression in different ways to my own. There's no such thing as one feminine truth. Gender, race, ethnicity, sexual orientation and socio-economic background intersect, and patriarchy is a system of oppression that underlies many other systems of oppression such as colonialism, racism, homophobia, elitism and classism.

Within the pages of this book, I have chosen to explore feminine power in the context of Western culture (with a few exceptions) because it's my own personal heritage. For clarity, when I refer to Western culture, I'm talking about Europe and continents colonised by Europeans such as Australasia and the Americas. The narrative I share here is only one small part of a much wider perspective of the feminine. So when you read this book, please bear in mind that this isn't the 'one' truth, but only a piece of a much more complicated puzzle.

Before I continue, I want to be explicit about my approach and attitudes towards 'feminism'. I do align myself with feminism but not necessarily in the traditional sense of the word. Mainstream feminism is a political movement aimed at establishing equal rights and protection for all women, although the majority of mainstream feminism up until now has been focused on the concerns of white women. It began in the 19th century and has seen many waves. The newest wave is intersectional feminism, which takes into account how gender intersects with other factors such as race, sexuality, class and socio-economic background. As a movement towards social justice, political feminism is completely necessary. Yet in my view, unless we're also doing the work to change our inner landscapes, fighting for the rights of all women can only go so far. Our internalised oppression is just as real as the external oppression.

It's my experience that when a woman changes how she feels about herself, she shows up differently. The patriarchal system is made up of people and we are part of it. The only way to create real social change is to change the system from the inside. That means embodying the change we wish to create. Without healing our feminine wounds and accessing our feminine power, we cannot truly create social and planetary justice. Feminism through the lens of both collective responsibility and personal responsibility becomes far more potent and effective at creating lasting social change. There must be space for duality. We must recognise that the system is fucked up and oppresses anyone who isn't a white cisgender male, and despite this, each of us, no matter what we've experienced, has the power and agency to change our individual and collective destiny.

The feminine hasn't always been treated as second-class. There's a huge body of evidence to show that, in European cultures of the past, the feminine was revered as sacred. Although there are many feminist books that have attempted to create a historical backdrop explaining life before patriarchy, I've found the majority that I have read to be disappointingly inaccurate and overgeneralised. Call it my academic training, but I believe that there is power in specificity, and the more we can pinpoint dates and places, the more we give weight to our argument — that patriarchy hasn't always been the way the world was ordered.

On a side note, when I refer to men and women, I'm referring to anyone who identifies with these genders. When I use the words masculine and feminine, I'm referring to archetypes, traits, energies and approaches. Regardless of the gender you identify with, feminine empowerment and the power of the priestess is available to you. It's here for everyone.

I'm also not here to blame men. First, it's not men's fault — we are all products of the systems we are born into. And second, continuing to play victim will not empower women. We do not need to blame men to reclaim feminine power. That said, men do have a responsibility to acknowledge their male privilege and to use it to create change. There are many men out there who abuse the patriarchal system and use it to wield power over others. They must be held accountable, which is why social movements such as the Me Too movement are just. I also believe that anger is an essential part of the women's rights movement — anger can be a righteous and effective power for those who feel their voices are not being heard. If women are getting angry, there's a reason for it and we must listen.

It's important to understand that the patriarchal system has also caused harm to people who identify as men because it's taught them that they must never be perceived as weak. That's a huge burden to carry. Yet, despite this trauma that patriarchy has inflicted upon men, the system is set up in a way that makes life for a man easier than life for a woman. Anyone who tries to dispute this is either a man or is a woman who is so indoctrinated into the patriarchal belief system that she's not aware of her own oppression.

So where does patriarchy come from? And why is it still so entrenched in our society today? I'm about to take you on a whistle-stop tour of patriarchy through the ages.

Ancient Greece is considered to be the birthplace of Western civilisation and up to and during the Early Bronze Age, at around 2000BC, the archaeological evidence suggests that there was equality between men and women. People across what is now known as Europe lived in small settlements and the scores of female clay figurines that litter archaeological sites across the Mediterranean suggest that these ancient people worshipped female fertility deities.

The Neolithic settlement of Çatalhöyük in modern-day Turkey is a fantastic example. This settlement flourished around 9000 years ago and the archaeology tells a striking story. Throughout the entire settlement, hundreds of clay figurines have been discovered, and what's fascinating is that nine out of ten of them are depictions of curvaceous females. It has been suggested that this may indicate a society whose religious ideology centred on the worship of the Divine Feminine. This is not to say that these cultures were a matriarchy, as some have argued, because there are depictions of men too. But it is evidence for a more egalitarian society, where men and women, the masculine and feminine, were treated as equal. And we can see similar archaeological evidence across much of Europe during the Neolithic and Early Bronze Age.

The strongest evidence that we do for a matriarchy, a society ruled by women, is on the island of Crete. The Minoan Civilisation flourished here between 1600 and 1500 BC and the archaeological evidence is striking and unique. In paintings and pottery, women are often depicted as seated in elaborate clothing, whereas men are often depicted as nude. It's rare that men are shown in positions of power. In the remains of Minoan palaces, there are also the remnants of ceremonial pits. In anthropological studies elsewhere, similar pits have been shown to be used as menstrual pits and so this is a possible interpretation, potentially indicating that women during their bleed time were treated with respect. If Minoan society was indeed matriarchal, it only lasted the span of a century or so before the island was conquered by armies from mainland Greece and the Minoan way of life was lost forever.

After 1600BC, society in the Mediterranean went through a huge socio-political shift that marked the beginning of the rise of male dominance and the decline of female power. Underpinning all of this was the shift towards a more capitalist society. With the blossoming of agricultural practices and the rapid development of crafts (that we take for granted today, such as metalworking, pottery and textiles), suddenly these societies had more resources available to them. And along with these new resources came the desire to secure and protect them.

A consequence of this was that, in the place of once peaceful agricultural settlements and citadels, huge fortifications were built, which signified the rise of militaristic culture. As the need to scare opponents and win wars increased, Gaia, mother of all the gods, was demoted, and suddenly the Greek pantheon found itself with a male godhead — Zeus, the formidable and fierce wielder of thunderbolts and fire. The religious preoccupation with male dominance trickled down into all crevices of society, and women — over the centuries — lost their power and autonomy.

By the fifth century BC, women were very much second-class citizens. Although the concept of democracy was developing during this time, women and slaves were left out of the conversation. Women had no political rights and were considered to be the property of their husbands. Most women were married soon after menarche (their first period) and grew up believing that their primary purpose was to bear children.

Archaeological and textual evidence suggests that the full disparity between male and female power did not take root until much later in other parts of Europe. Prior to the Roman invasion of Ancient Britain, women held positions of power and prestige, as shown by female chariot 'warrior' burials dating to 2500BC discovered in the north of England. And according to the Roman writer, Tacitus, in the first century BC, the infamous warrior Queen, Boudicca, led her people to revolt against Roman imperialism (but lost). Once the Romans had managed to fully occupy Britain a century later, tribal culture diminished, and with it, feminine status was lost. Boudicca has now since become immortalised as a symbol of ancient feminine power.

ANCIENT PRIESTESSHOOD

In and around the Mediterranean, although women, in general, were taught to know their place, there were women, just like Boudicca, who chose to defy the status quo. None were more famous than the poetess Sappho.

Born in the sixth century BC to an aristocratic family on the Greek island of Lesbos, Sappho was an icon in the ancient world and her legacy has endured even today. Her poetry speaks about the ecstasy of love and deep sensuality. In particular, she speaks of the love between women, which is why the word lesbian comes from the name of her island home, Lesbos.

Sappho is an enigma of the ancient world, partially because what remains of her poetry is fragmentary (much of it was destroyed in later centuries by the Christian Church for being salacious) and partly because, despite there being no overwhelming evidence, many believe that she was, in fact, a priestess. Indeed many of her poems pay homage to the pagan goddess Aphrodite.

Although we don't know for sure that Sappho was a priestess, history tells us of other female poets who were openly practicing their priesthood. Enheduanna, who lived at around 2250BC in what's now modern-day Iraq, is one of the first recorded female writers. She was the daughter of King Sargon of Akkad, and he gave Enheduanna the position of high priestess — a political move to maintain power in the region. As priestess, she composed many hymns of praise to the goddess Ishtar. In her moving poetry, she contemplates the formidable power of the warrior goddess Ishtar and what it is to be female.

As the centuries marched on, and as women's power in ancient society decreased, priesthood became a doorway to increased status and civil rights. In Ancient Greece, at around the eighth century BC, the most famous position of priestesshood was the oracle of Delphi, known as the Pythia. High priestess of the god Apollo, the Pythia's role in ancient Greek society was to dispense advice and wisdom to people from all walks of life. Ordinary people would consult her for commentary on matters related to daily civilian life. Political leaders would consult her about state affairs. In the role of Pythia, the woman in question had immense influence and power and, in a world dominated by men, it's ironic to reflect that the most powerful person in the ancient world was actually a woman. Her wisdom was thought to be channelled from the god Apollo himself and, as such, the Pythia could say whatever she wanted without consequence.

Priestesshood endured throughout the centuries. In ancient Rome, from the seventh century BC onwards, the sacred flame of the city was kept burning by a group of priestesses known as the Vestal Virgins. Priestesses of Vesta, goddess of the home, they were selected during childhood and were usually from aristocratic backgrounds. The duty of these priestesses was to keep the sacred fire of Rome burning — an immensely prestigious honour. It was believed that if the fire went out, Rome would meet its demise. They were also to stay chaste during their thirty years of service and wore elaborate wedding gowns, signifying their union to Rome itself. In return, the Vestals were given almost goddess-like status and were free from the social obligation to marry or bear children.

Their situation wasn't empowering in the true sense of the word. Being a Vestal wasn't easy and young girls were primed for this role before they had a real say in their lives. In times of crisis, Vestals were used as scapegoats — their chastity would be questioned and their alleged crimes punished. Rome was essentially policing the bodies of these women by forcing them to refrain from sexual activity and conditioning them to believe that, if they were to stray, they were committing treason against Rome itself. If a Vestal did succumb to her natural impulses, there was no mercy. In 483BC, Oppia, a Vestal, was found guilty of allegedly having had sexual relations. She was entombed alive, condemned to experience a lonely, terrifying death.

The Vestal Virgins, to my mind, represent a state's desire to have power over its women through religion. These women did not have true autonomy over their lives. They were slaves to the system. Yet, as priestesses, they were given social status and prestige that ordinary women did not have access to. They could own property. They could vote. They were entrusted with important state documents. And once they retired from the priestesshood, they continued to benefit from elevated social status. Despite what it cost them, these women were immensely respected. They were central to religious ceremony, and they simultaneously kept the fire of Rome burning for nearly 1000 years and immortalised themselves in the pages of history.

You wouldn't think it now, but priestesshood also played a huge role in the spread of Early Christianity. In 50AD, Christianity was but a small group of people who had branched off from traditional Judaism. Led by Paul in what is now modern-day Turkey, they had a mission to spread Christianity throughout the Roman Empire. Ironically, for a faith that's now so patriarchal in its structure, during its infancy, it was women who were spreading the message of Christ. In fact, during the first two centuries AD, roughly half of new churches were founded by women. This was the time during which to be a Christian in Rome was to be a criminal. And still, women felt called to be part of and to teach this radical new faith.

The second-century text known as 'The Acts of Paul and Thecla' is not included in the Bible and yet it's an important source for understanding the role that women played in the spread and adoption of Early Christianity. Thecla was a 13-year-old girl living in Iconium (Turkey). After hearing Paul giving a sermon, she was hooked. She disobeyed her parents by bribing the guards to let her out so she could sit at Paul's feet all night, listening to his teachings. His message captivated her. When they were discovered, Thecla's mother was enraged and ordered that Thecla be burned to death. But Thecla managed to escape to reunite with Paul. They hit the road together and she became one of Paul's most loyal followers.

The initial message of Christianity was that the world was ending soon and this opened up huge opportunities for women. Their primary social responsibility as women was to bear children, but now there was no need. As a consequence, they chose to take a much more active role in the Early Christian Church.

It's hard to believe, given the way the Catholic Church is structured today, but in the first few centuries of Christianity, women led worship and shared the teachings of Christ. We can see this very clearly in the archaeology — in the Catacombs of Priscilla in Rome, painted figures on the walls clearly depict ordained priestesses and women in positions of religious leadership. In the Early Christian Church, women were handmaidens of God and, as a consequence, held positions of power and authority.

This all changed in the 4th century AD because of one man: Augustine of Hippo, born in Numidia, a Roman Province in Algeria. According to his own biography, he had a colourful youth, consorting with prostitutes and concubines. But later, he turned over a new leaf and became a bishop of the Christian Church. It was Augustine who promoted the concept of original sin — the idea that the sin of humanity originates from the moment Eve persuaded Adam to eat the forbidden apple, which then prompted God to kick them out of the Garden of Eden. Augustine very much held women responsible for bringing original sin into the world and for being a continuing source of seduction. He also taught that pleasurable sex was despicable and dirty. What a guy.

Augustine's anti-women narrative was the straw that broke the camel's back for women's role within the Christian Church. In the fourth century, it was decreed that women could no longer be priestesses. And soon after, all pagan worship was outlawed and the temples to the gods and goddesses of old were demolished. As a consequence, the feminine and the role of women in religious worship were completely obliterated.

Christianity had initially opened up portals to women to embody their priestesshood and live their Divine purpose, but within a few centuries, this had been stripped away. Despite there being an imbalance in power between ordinary men and women for thousands of years, up until the 4th century AD, priestesses were essential to religion and therefore central to life. In priestesshood, these women had found a way to reclaim their power and worth.

OPPRESSION, REBELLION AND PERSECUTION

In the centuries that followed, women may not have been allowed to officially lead religious worship, but they were still undoubtedly practicing their priestesshood elsewhere in secret, as healers and teachers. The patriarchal system punished them for it and they were hunted down. Witch hysteria in Europe began in the 1400s but swept across the continent fiercely in the sixteenth and seventeenth centuries. It's estimated that between 40,000 to 60,000 people were put on trial and executed for witchcraft, the majority of whom were single women, widows, and those who lived on the margins of society. It's likely that most of these women were misunderstood 'wise women' who used traditional herbal knowledge and harmless pagan spells.

During this time, the general population grew to be incredibly suspicious and fearful. What was once seen as harmless pagan superstition became the scapegoat for collective fear. Witches were branded as consorts of the Devil and, as a consequence, once they'd been found guilty, they were condemned to be either burned at the stake or hanged. During the witch hunts, confessions were usually obtained through horrendous torture practices. Our ancestors didn't stand a chance and my blood runs cold to even think about the trauma that they endured.

The Witch Trials of the sixteenth and seventeenth centuries have undoubtedly left a deep and heavy imprint in the feminine psyche. We still fear the judgement. We still fear persecution. And yet we also still crave to embody the priestess, no matter what.

Colonialism has played a huge part in the global spread of the patriarchal system of oppression. This was led by the Portuguese and Spanish in the 1500s, who conquered vast parts of the Americas, the Middle East, India and Asia. The Dutch and English followed suit in the sixteenth and seventeenth centuries, competing with each other to grow their empires. The pages of history often report these facts dryly and without emotion and yet whenever I think of colonisation, I can't help but imagine the horror experienced by indigenous communities who had their land, their rights and their way of life stripped away from them. Back then, white supremacy, a system of oppression that benefits people of white skin colour, was very much rooted in the patriarchal ideology that elevated the white affluent male. The sad fact is that this system of oppression still operates globally today, in both obvious and subtle ways.

It's clear to me that women in today's world very much feel a strong pull towards the priestess. Some may call it their inner witchiness or their inner 'woo' — but it's the same energy — an ancient remembering of feminine sovereignty. And in a world that still continues to devalue the feminine, invoking the priestess is the route to the reclamation of our individual and collective power and balance.

The patriarchal system has tried to shut down our priesshood. But now we are answering the call to take it back because women have always yearned to walk hand in hand with the Divine. We feel it because we are Divinity incarnate.

How do we reclaim our feminine power and divinity? How do we come home to our authentic selves, reclaim our feminine magic, share our voices, own our gifts, and create a life of freedom? How do we move beyond the toxic stories that we tell ourselves about not being good enough, experienced enough, or qualified enough to make a difference? How do we unapologetically channel our priesshood into something tangible and powerful, be it a thriving business, a non-profit or a movement? And how, as women, do we build lives that are deeply satisfying and fulfilling? My intention is that you will find the answers to these questions within the pages of this book. Throughout our time together, I'll be taking you on a journey, stopping at four destinations: illumination, reclamation, revelation, and emancipation.

Our journey of feminine empowerment always begins with illumination. We cannot break free from our prison if we're unable to see its walls. This means we must understand the external systems of oppression and internal narratives that have been keeping women small, stuck and chained. Patriarchy has a lot to answer for and when we understand the ways in which its limiting narratives have been deeply etched into the fabric of who we think we are, it becomes a lot easier to have self-compassion. As we learn to let go of our shame, we create space and free up energy for ourselves to thrive.

The journey continues with reclamation. When we choose to be brave, we activate our ability to live in radically new ways. Reclamation is the process of reconnecting to our true authentic selves and our potent feminine magic. It's about honouring our creative and intuitive superpowers. As this happens, we start to recognise and embody our self-worth and, as a result, it becomes easier to fully experience the joy and ecstasy of life.

With this comes revelation and hearing the ways in which the priestess speaks to us and wants to be channelled. The process of revelation is the point at which we begin to acknowledge and own our skills, our talents, our gifts and where we begin making the brave decision to channel them into something tangible. As this happens, we become clearer on what we're here for and what we're no longer available for.

And finally, this leads us to emancipation. We choose to reject the limiting systems that we have inherited and free ourselves up to live lives that turn us on. We choose to bravely express ourselves unapologetically and make decisions that are in alignment with our deep desires. We start acting. We start channelling. We put our gifts out into the world. We follow our callings. We allow ourselves to thrive: emotionally, spiritually and financially. We use our power to create heaven here on earth. We become champions for justice, fairness and healing. We create the change we wish to see in the world. And we liberate the feminine in the process. This is the way of the priestess.

ILLUMINATE & TRANSCEND
End of Chapter Contemplations

At the end of each chapter, you will find a collection of contemplative prompts. Contemplation is the process of bringing something into our awareness and allowing the light of our consciousness to reveal the layers of its meaning to us time and time again. It encourages true transformation by providing space for us to gain deeper clarity on our insights and to integrate them into our lives.

You can contemplate through journalling or by going for a walk in nature and asking yourself the question over and over again.

Don't rush through this process. Give yourself space and time for the wisdom to emerge and you'll be blown away by what you discover.

Here are the contemplative prompts for this chapter:

- *Why did you pick up this book?*

- *What do you feel is calling you?*

- *What are you yearning for?*

- *What has resonated with you already?*

- *What has already transformed within you by choosing to read this book?*

ILLUMINATION

Understanding the toxicity of patriarchy allows us to recognise what we're dealing with so that rather than beating ourselves up, we get to take a look at the ways in which experiences throughout our lives have shaped what we believe about ourselves and the habitual ways in which we respond. It's only when we illuminate something fully that we can then transcend it.

The journey of feminine empowerment must include the process of illumination. We cannot break free from our prison if we're unable to see its walls. The patriarchal system has a lot to answer for and when we understand what we're dealing with, the path to liberation becomes clearer. In this part of the book, through the narrative of my own story, I share with you how patriarchy keeps women prisoner and how we can set ourselves free.

LIVING WITH PARADOX

I've lost count of the number of women who've told me that they feel stuck and stagnant in their current life situations and that they know they're being called to make a real difference and play truer. Yet, despite this inner knowing, they're unable to take the leap. And this was certainly my experience throughout my twenties.

As I progressed in my academic career and learned more about ancient ways of living, it's not surprising that I chose to write my doctorate about the European Bronze Age, an era that was unmarked by the oppressive nature of patriarchy. It's also not a shock that I began to feel that the archaic structure of academia itself was oppressing the very feminine essence I was so keen to reconnect to. The paradox was that, as I tumbled further down the academic rabbit hole, I found myself living out the narrative of patriarchy on a micro-scale. The foundations of academia — white supremacy, elitism, competition and hierarchy — seemed to me to mirror the underpinnings of patriarchy itself.

And whilst I sat in this ivory tower, every day I found myself questioning why I'd been taught to research and write without emotion, why I had to use academic jargon that most people wouldn't understand, and why I was supposed to work long hours and crank out publications like my life depended upon it.

I realised I was close to burnout. And, in addition, it was painfully obvious to me that, within the fabric of academia itself, there was and still is, inherent discrimination against women and other marginalised groups. Despite there being a huge number of female postgraduates within my department, the number of female professors was sorely disproportionate to the number of males. And there were notably no women of colour in positions of leadership in our faculty.

Within my second year as a PhD researcher, I had made my assessment: academia was an ivory tower of elitism that kept knowledge (and therefore power) with a chosen few. It also urged women to act like men or fail. I knew deep down in the marrow of my bones that my purpose in life was more expansive. But I was unable to translate this inner knowing into the action of leaving. And so I stumbled on.

DISCOVERING YOGA

I discovered yoga at the age of 19. Or maybe it's more accurate to state that yoga found me. Yoga is a set of physical, mental and spiritual practices that cultivate harmony and union between body, mind and spirit. I stumbled across it quite by accident and never looked back. My first teacher was a beautiful Indian woman called Meeta. She was as bendy as a pretzel and fiercely devoted to her practice and teaching. I then came across my teacher Satyananda and studied with him for years.

I loved it. To me, it felt like coming home. Admittedly, there was part of me that initially felt uncomfortable about the practice of yoga and the blatant appropriation of Indian culture — I had never been to India and it was weird to be suddenly chanting in Sanskrit and learning about Hindu gods and goddesses, particularly because I'm British and the barbaric way in which Britain colonised India is something that will always turn my stomach. And yet, in yoga, I found a modality for bringing myself back to my centre and returning to my truest essence.

I became fascinated with the teachings and origins of yoga. I learned that yoga, as it's practiced today, is a blend of ancient teachings and nineteenth-century British gymnastics (it's argued that British missionaries actually influenced the formation of specific yoga traditions such as Ashtanga).

And as I went deeper down the yogic rabbit hole, I also contemplated why it was that I had had to search outside of my own culture for modalities to bring me closer to my true self. To my mind at least, it became clear that when Christianity outlawed paganism 1500 or so years ago, our own ancient spiritual practices died. The incorporation of yoga into my life felt like a spiritual reclamation. And it paved the way for a spiritual unfolding that encouraged me to start to reawaken the priestess. Although there are many aspects of the Western adoption of yoga that I find incredibly problematic — mainly the focus being on skinny white women who perform circus tricks for social media likes — at its core is a universal message: we are all Divine and we are powerful beyond measure. This is the power of the priestess.

WAKING UP

My whole world changed at the age of 24. I was in the second year of my PhD candidacy and it was a sunny winter's day in Zagreb, Croatia. I was there spending a few weeks collecting data for my thesis. This particular day was a Saturday and I decided to head over to an art museum to get out of research mode and see something different.

As I was walking around the museum, squinting to make sense of the contemporary installations, I felt my phone vibrate in my bag. And when I checked it a few minutes later, I saw that I had a message from my Dad.

'Bad news about Nev. Ring as soon as you can.'

Nev was my brother. Well, half-brother actually, but that didn't make a difference. Older than me by nine years, I idolised him as a child. He was a troubled man and our whole family history can be summed up as multiple episodes of estrangements followed by periods of closeness and healing. During his teenage years and twenties, he'd had several run-ins with the law. But in recent years it had seemed that he'd finally gotten his life straightened out. He was engaged. He was working in a job that he loved. He was following his calling to create music.

Feeling my heart beating in my chest, I rushed as quickly as I could to the exit and found myself a step to sit on. Phone shaking in my hand, I called my parents, but before they even answered, I already knew.

During that call, I learned that he had died from an accidental drug overdose, at a party, on a canal boat, surrounded by fear and confusion. Thirty-three years old and gone.

This was the only time in my entire life I have ever witnessed my dad cry. I was numb with shock. To me this felt like the kind of thing that happened to other people. Not to me. Not to my family.

I flew back to England to be with my parents and my younger brother, Tom, that same day. I don't remember anything about the journey other than the fact that I deeply wished that someone at the airport, anyone, would come and hug me as I waited for my flight. All I wanted in that moment was the comfort of a stranger's embrace. No-one met my gaze.

I spent the following three weeks at my family home and it was incredibly hard. I wanted to sleep and never wake up, but I couldn't. I knew I had to be the strong one because everyone else seemed to be falling apart. My mother was in shock. My dad couldn't even bring himself to arrange the funeral. I took on responsibilities during that week that I was not ready for. I simply did what I had to do.

As the days went by, we were able to slowly piece together what had happened. The toxicology report showed that it was a 'legal high' that had killed him. And as we spoke to his friends and fiancée, we learned that Nev had had a ketamine addiction. The tragedy was that he had been clean for almost a year.

I'd had no idea. I felt so stupid and so naive. The next few weeks were agony. Grief is a powerful force to be reckoned with and if you haven't been prepared for it, which I hadn't, it knocks you to the ground.

I had two choices: Continue to suppress, or deeply feel.

And so I gave myself over to the process. I dived headfirst into messy grief. I let the pain come, wave after wave. Because there was a deeper wisdom inside of me, whispering: 'this will be your liberator.' And it was.

Within ten months I was reborn. Not only had the pain of grief taught my numb and closed heart how to feel, but through its transformative energy, I had no choice but to face the truth I had been too scared to confront —- that I was not living in alignment with my soul purpose and it was time to make some changes.

THAILAND

It's been ten months since Nev's passing and I'm on a white sandy beach in Thailand. It's about 4am. Shooting stars are darting across the twinkling sky and the moon is about to set into the ocean.

I feel a sting of guilt thinking about my boyfriend back in England but it feels unbelievably good to be lying here in the arms of Canadian Dan. Don't get me wrong, it's not that this guy is my one true love. But he smells good, his kisses taste like tequila, and talking to him this evening has helped me to remember who I really am.

We met one boozy night in Bangkok (I have vague memories of us dancing on the bar, singing John Denver songs). He then followed me to Koh Phangan. We've just spent the past four hours chatting non-stop with each other about our lives. I've poured out my life story to him. And I've admitted to him something that I've never dared admit to myself before, let alone to anyone else: that I want to leave the UK and teach yoga. The cocktails may have gone to my head but, in many ways, I've never felt clearer in my life.

For the past month, I've been traveling around Thailand with my friend. It was supposed to be an 'Eat Pray Love' kind of trip. I envisaged us doing yoga on the beach every morning and drinking green smoothies. But Thailand had other ideas for us. We've spent the past month in a maelstrom of catharsis. Party after party. Drink after drink. Flirtation. Dancing. Wildness. I feel liberated in a way I've never felt before. Here I'm not someone's daughter or girlfriend. I'm not the sensible PhD student who's trying to fit herself into a box in which she doesn't belong. I'm just Sarah.

A few days after the romantic evening with Canadian Dan, I find myself boarding my flight back to the UK. I cry on and off for pretty much the whole flight, not because of Dan (I'd pretty much forgotten about him), but because I know I have to radically change my life. And I'm so scared.

On returning, I managed fairly quickly to find the bravery to break-up with my boyfriend of six years. Or perhaps it's more accurate to say that life gave me no alternative. The day after I returned home, as I was lying in bed questioning my very existence, that sweet innocent man got down on one knee and proposed to me. Every cell in my body screamed at me to say no. And so I turned him down. I will never forget the look on his face as he quickly put the ring away. But nor will I forget the feeling of relief that flooded my body. It was the first time in a long time that I had made a decision where I was being more loyal to my authentic desires than to my fear.

At 18 years old, we were just kids when we met. We fell in love quickly and he was my rock. But as the years went on, I started to crave more. I didn't care that he didn't have a high-level job or a flashy car. What I craved was a deeper connection. We only seemed to be able to connect over festivals and pints, but I wanted more depth. The truth is that we should have broken up years earlier than we did. In our sixth and final year of the relationship, I was already starting to pull away. But I could never quite bring myself to sever the ties. I wanted to have my cake and to eat it — I simply couldn't choose between the safety of him and the excitement of the unknown. And because of my paralysis, I left him dangling: enslaved in a relationship that was nourishing neither of us.

Leaving him wasn't a walk in the park but it hurt a lot less than I thought it would. The next break-up I had to face was with my career. I wanted to follow my true calling but I was having trouble taking the leap. I knew I had no choice but to leave my life as an academic and follow a deeper, truer calling. My connection with the priestess was reactivated. But I was still too paralysed with fear to follow it.

THE PRIESTESS CALLS

When referring to my connection to the priestess, I use the word 'reactivate' intentionally. The priestess wasn't unknown to me. She's not unknown to any of us. I'd already heard her call but I was choosing to ignore her message.

I first met her at the age of 15. My mum's best friend had given me an oracle deck, and there she was on the cover — Dana, the High Priestess — hauntingly beautiful and immensely powerful. Looking into her eyes offered me a glimpse into a world that I knew deep down but had long forgotten.

By the age of 16, I was dabbling in goddess worship. I would whisper to the moon, talk to the trees and feel the feminine spirit all around me. By day, our family garden was where we enjoyed barbecues and summer lunches. By night, it was my sacred space where I would engage in magic ritual and connect to the energy of my ancestors. Tom watched from his upper bedroom window, sniggering but also curious.

There's no doubt about it: I was the 'weird kid'. I listened to punk, I questioned authority, I drank and danced under the stars. I kissed who I wanted to kiss and felt so alive. I hated school. I didn't fit it. I didn't belong. I wasn't lazy and I wanted to learn. It's just that I instinctively felt that the school system was restrictive and oppressive. My feminine spirit, so curious and expansive, wanted to dance free and explore. But the heaviness of school conditioning finally won and, seeing how proud it made everyone, I finally abandoned my free spirit to go to university and study archaeology. I did this partly because it was an avenue for connecting with the past but also because it was an option that matched a subconscious drive to please others and do what was expected of me.

And so, at the age of 24, after years of hustling to prove myself and trying to be something that deep down I wasn't, I was finally ready to reclaim my truth and embody the priestess. However, the transition wasn't swift or easy.

It seems to me that, in our modern world, almost every single structure — be it social, political, economic or academic — is built to shut out a woman's priestesshood. In these structures, there's no room for a woman's intuition, a woman's emotionality, or a woman's compassion. In short, there's no space for a woman's true power. In order to succeed, a woman is taught that she has to suppress, downplay, or apologise for her feminine magic. A woman is gaslighted and told that the struggles she sees playing out in the world aren't real or aren't that bad, and that her anger isn't warranted. As such, a woman is taught not to speak up or speak out against her own sense of personal injustice and not to mention the injustices that she sees in this fucked-up world.

As a result, whilst finishing up my PhD and getting ready to leave it all behind, I felt like I had a split personality. On one hand, I was still going through the motions of my academic life, on the other hand, I was going through my yoga teacher training, chanting in Sanskrit and reading every self-development book I could.

I fervently hid my witchiness from colleagues, terrified of judgement or not being taken seriously. But conversely, as a product of my conditioning, I also found myself rolling my eyes at any spiritual theories that, for me, were a little bit too 'out there'. For months, I found myself in a liminal space and I didn't know where I belonged or what my real role or purpose was. The trip to Thailand gave me greater clarity but I was still unsure what to do next. Fear was keeping me prisoner, even though the jail door was open.

I needn't have fretted about it. It turns out that the universe had a plan for me. And, despite the fact that outwardly things over the next couple of years appeared to get worse before they got better, everything was unfolding for me beautifully. It turns out all I needed to do was surrender to the mystery and follow the breadcrumbs.

SAFE AT LAST

Several years later, I'm sat on the bedroom floor of the villa I'm renting in Portugal. It's late evening and it feels as if the sadness I'm feeling might swallow me whole. To be honest, I'm not even sure that I want to live. I have never felt so lost and so alone.

A few weeks previously, I'd boarded a one-way flight to the western Algarve in search of inner peace and a fresh start. It had taken me a while to find a place to live and my job prospects for teaching yoga full-time weren't great, but I was finally starting to feel safe in this sleepy and forgotten corner of Europe. I guess I had an intuitive knowing that my soul was supposed to be here.

Except that right now, as I'm crouched on the floor doing the ugly cry, it feels like anything but destiny. It's all hit me and I'm letting it out. Finally.

You're safe, Sarah, you're safe.

Because, although I had been pretending to the world otherwise, the truth was, I'd been living a lie. Sat there, crumpled on the cold tiled floor, memories flash before my eyes.

Being pinned up against the wall of the shower, his forearm crushing my throat...Trying to scream but no sound coming out — my windpipe and vocal cords sealed shut by the strength of his grip...The terrifying thought 'this is how I die' popping into my head again and again... Me hoping our neighbours would come and save me... The sickening sound of my skull smacking the wall and the shock as I watched the blood spill from my forehead and mix with the water on the bathroom floor... Sitting together, hugging and crying at the horror of it all... My forehead being sewn up with three big ugly stitches...

But now I am safe. Safe.

RED FLAGS AND SELF-BETRAYAL

I'd met him only a few months after coming back from Thailand. After my recent break-up, I was feeling more magnetic and more confident than ever before. I was learning how to be single and learning that I really liked my own company. Which is of course when I met him — I swear some guys are only interested when a woman poses more of a challenge.

The red flags were there right from the beginning of the relationship. Love bombing. Subtle contempt and control. The knot in my stomach that something wasn't right. I brushed it all aside. In fact, I gaslighted myself. I told myself to be more compassionate. I told myself it wasn't a big deal. I told myself the universe had clearly brought us together for a reason. I told myself how lucky I was to have a guy who loved me so much, so quickly.

As time went on, the red flags became bigger and more in my face. The smashing of my property. Put-downs. The swallowing of tears. I began to fear the nights he'd go out drinking with the lads because shit often went down afterwards. But still, I didn't leave him.

In response, a few years in, I started to have liaisons with others guys — nothing physical — but just enough of an emotional connection to rouse his suspicion and jealousy.

And so we carried on, caught in a web of toxicity that neither of us were brave enough to escape from. I told myself that, sure he had anger issues, but he'd never hurt me physically. Never.

But that wasn't the case and he did hurt me. I still have the scar on my forehead, forever reminding me of the pent-up anger and rage that came flooding out of him one terrifying evening. And yet, despite having feared for my life, I chose to stay with him.

It wasn't the abuse that hurt me so much, it was my own self-betrayal. I hated lying to everyone about what had happened — I knew no-one believed my 'I slipped in the shower story' anyway. And I felt like a statistic I had never asked to become. I was also a fraud: I was teaching feminine empowerment in my yoga classes when the reality was that I was the poster girl for disempowerment.

After that violent night, the relationship turned even more toxic than I could have imagined. Within a few weeks, it was becoming increasingly difficult to hang around with my friends without provoking his anger. And because I was terrified of him, I found myself lying to him, pleading with him and apologising to him. I did anything to keep the peace.

The periods of drama and despair were always followed by periods of bliss. He was sweet. He took care of me. He talked about marriage and kids. I couldn't help it: I was hooked. My logical mind was disgusted at what I was allowing myself to become, but he was like a drug — the more he pulled away from me, the more I wanted him.

A few weeks after the attack, he turned violent again and, fearing for my life, I ran from him and stayed at my friend's house. I told her everything and it was agreed that, in the morning, I'd go to my place, pack a bag and come and stay with her. I meant to, I really did, but as soon as I saw him, I succumbed. I pleaded with him and told him I'd do better. And after that, I started seeing my friends much less. They were worried but what could they do? They knew that I wasn't ready to face the truth and they had the foresight to recognise that they couldn't push me — I had to come to the conclusion myself.

But none of that matters now. I've finally left. Here, alone in

Portugal, I'm sat on the floor, clutching my phone and searching for comfort as I read the encouraging messages from my friends back in the UK. All the pain, all the pent-up trauma, all the relief...it's oozing out of me in the form of uncontrollable sobs and big fat tears. Another sleepless night awaits me.

GASLIGHTING

I'm 30 and I've just received an email from my ex, telling me that he's going to take legal action against me regarding a blog post I've written about my experience of domestic abuse and violence.

I'm in complete shock. My body is shaking. I reread his words.

'Your representation of events is deranged.'

I begin retching. And that's where I begin to question myself. Again. What if I was making it out to be worse than it was? The knee-jerk reaction to edit myself, deny my truth and pull the blog post down is incredibly strong. Years ago that is exactly what I would have done. But not this time.

I let myself shake and cry and vomit. Then I web search for a lawyer who specialises in domestic violence cases and fire her an email. Her response fortifies me with a sense of resolve. She tells me that there was nothing damning in my blog post, that I don't need to take it down, and that she suspects nothing will come of this threat because she's seen situations like this many times before. Despite her words, I can't eat a thing that evening. I'm on high alert. Waiting.

Once I had fully left the relationship, I realised that I didn't need to lie anymore. I could, if I was brave enough, speak the truth. So I started to candidly share about my experience, with one woman, and then another. My sharing not only became medicine for me but also medicine for the sisterhood. I've lost count of the number of women who have responded to my story with 'me too'.

Domestic abuse and violence are unfathomably present in

today's society and the statistics are frightening. A high percentage of women who are killed know their murderers and an alarming number of the perpetrators are either their partners or ex-partners. This is much higher than the number of men killed by their partners. Choosing to stay in a relationship that has become violent is dangerous. It only takes one punch or one shove for a 'tragic accident' to occur. I know this from personal experience. That night, as he was attempting to squeeze the life out of me, I was completely at his mercy. The truth is that he could have killed me. And what then? Would he have been held accountable? Would he have managed to convince a jury that it was a crime of passion? Would I have been another woman whose precious life was ended far too soon?

Often when I share my story, I see him as a faceless entity. To me, he represents a phenomenon and my decision to share was never about victimising myself or demonising him as a perpetrator. I simply wanted to tell the truth because I believe that the truth is our liberator. The light of truth casts out shame, and it's my belief that shame is the very fuel that gets us into, and keeps us in, these toxic situations in the first place.

When I started sharing my experience on social media, it really pissed him off. I was always careful not to name him of course, but he felt victimised. He threatened me. Members of his family sent me messages. They never understood that the telling of my story was never about him. It was about me. I was simply telling the story that far too many women globally have experienced but never shared.

When I originally sat down to write about the horrors of what happened that night, I wrote it as a passage full of rich detail — where, when and how. It felt incredibly liberating to finally own it in all its messiness and rawness. As I sat at my kitchen table, finishing up the final sentence, a wave of relief flowed through me. It felt like the last time I would ever need to share it — I wanted it out there in the world, helping women own their stories and make empowering choices.

But, after much agonising reflection, I chose to include a more watered-down and edited version of events. I cannot share with you the dark and twisted details of my experience without opening myself up to the possibility of a lawsuit, should he be identifiable. I've even deleted pictures of us together on my social media, just in case.

I chose this because I have seen too many women let down by a judicial system that is rigged against its women. I do not trust that the system would protect me, even though I was the one who was violently assaulted. I have a friend who was made by law to testify against her abusive ex-boyfriend in California and not only did she lose, but she was branded a liar and a fraud. Sadly, her story is far from unique and I don't want that for myself. Instead, I've chosen to tell my story differently. I edit myself to stay safe — it's what women have been doing for millennia.

And despite feeling a niggling sense of disappointment towards myself for doing so, I stand by this choice. To publish the sordid details and risk him being identified would be an act of self-betrayal and self-sabotage. I'm deeply happy and content with the life I've created for myself since I left him. And I will not allow that to be threatened. Because I deserve safety. I deserve peace. I deserve to breathe freely.

The truth is that, in many ways, I still feel love for him and the wonderful man he was underneath all of his pain. Is it love or is it a trauma-bond? Trauma bonds are a strong emotional attachment between an abused person and their abuser. These are formed as a result of the cycle of violence. And perhaps this is what I'm still feeling, even to this day. All I know is that I forgave him a long time ago and the sharing of this particular story has never been about retribution. It's instead a cautionary tale for any of you reading this who recognise yourself in my story. My message is clear: get out before you get hurt.

WHY STRONG WOMEN STAY

We find ourselves in the patterns of denial when we feel intense shame. But denial and lying also reinforce shame, and it was this, not the abuse, that eroded my sense of self and left me feeling utterly exhausted and disempowered.

The number one question that haunts all abused women is: 'why didn't you leave him sooner?' I wish I could answer that in a short succinct sentence, but the truth is multi-faceted and deeply complex.

I stayed for a myriad of reasons: I downplayed my experience; I felt love for him; I believed I needed him. And the number one reason? I was scared.

The typical portrayal of a domestic abuse victim is that they are weak and meek. But this couldn't be further from the truth. These situations are usually a complicated concoction of psychological warfare, trauma responses and social conditioning.

He was my lover and my abuser. My brain was unable to comprehend this conflict. And so I did what all 'good girls' are conditioned to do in the face of messiness or confusion: pretend you didn't see anything and act like it wasn't a big deal.

Women are socially conditioned to ignore red flags. The term 'gaslighting' refers to the denial of a person's reality and can manifest in all relationships, but particularly intimate ones. But the research is clear: gaslighting is rooted in social inequality related to race, nationality, sexual orientation and gender. It affects far more women than men and it begins at an early age. This is not to say that men don't experience abuse, but social inequality makes women and other marginalised groups far more likely to be subjected to it. Specifically related to gender, femininity is still associated with irrationality (the word 'hysteria', coined in the 19th century to describe exaggerated emotional agitation, comes from the ancient Greek 'hystera', meaning womb). This bias is often used against victims to erode their reality. We see it in the caricature of the 'irrational woman' or the stereotype of the 'angry black woman'.

Gaslighting was there in our childhood whenever we were told that we were making a fuss out of nothing, that it wasn't that bad, that we misunderstood and that we remembered wrong. It was happening any time an authority figure made us feel stupid for asking obvious questions or questioning what we were being told. Of course, questioning the status quo and what's considered as normal is one of our greatest superpowers and, as empowered women, we must learn to question the hell out of everything that doesn't feel right. But as little girls, we were taught that to ask for clarity is a sign of stupidity, and the last thing we wanted was to be called a stupid little girl.

When it comes to the reclamation of our feminine power, we must understand that the reason that we doubt ourselves is not our fault (even though the world has tried to convince us that it is) — it's a response to bias and discrimination against the feminine. This has conditioned us to question our perception of reality.

We only have to look at the world stage to see that the devaluation of the feminine plays out on a macro scale. When Donald Trump was sworn into The White House, I felt like the wind had been knocked out of me. Here was someone who had been recorded saying overtly misogynistic and degrading remarks, and yet, no doubt because of his corrupt campaign, had still been voted into the White House. The lack of consequence for his lewd behaviour sent a very clear message to women globally: the world does not respect you.

Understanding this toxicity allows us to recognise what we're dealing with so that rather than beating ourselves up and believing we are weak or useless, we get to take a look at the ways in which experiences throughout our lives have shaped what we believe about ourselves and the habitual ways in which we respond. Because it's only when we illuminate something fully that we can then transcend it.

I wasn't able to access the priestess during the dark years with my ex. My relationship back then was like a swamp of quicksand — the more I tried to break myself free, the deeper I sank. Even though the priestess was whispering to me during this time, I was unable to converse with her. As women, we can't live our divine purpose whilst we are trying to fix another or save ourselves. When we are in such depths of darkness, we forget that we deserve to shine.

ILLUMINATE & TRANSCEND
End of Chapter Contemplations

Contemplation is the process of bringing something into our awareness and allowing the light of our consciousness to reveal the layers of its meaning to us time and time again. It encourages true transformation by providing space for us to gain deeper clarity on our insights and integrate them into our lives.

You can contemplate through journalling or by going for a walk in nature and asking yourself the question over and over again.

Don't rush through this process. Give yourself space and time for the wisdom to emerge and you'll be blown away by what you discover.

Here are the contemplative prompts for this chapter:

- What really resonated with you throughout these pages?

- Where do you see yourself in Sarah's story?

- What have been your biggest breakthrough realisations so far?

RECLAMATION

It takes a truly brave woman to commit to connecting to and honouring her true self, especially when the social pressure to be someone else is incredibly strong, which it always is. But it's the only way to live a joyful and liberated life. It's the only way to reclaim our power and reveal our divine purpose. It's the only way to live as the priestess.

Our journey continues with reclamation. When we choose to be brave, we activate our ability to live in radically new ways. Reclamation is the process of reconnecting to our true authentic self and our potent feminine magic. It's about honouring our creative, intuitive superpowers and self-worth. In this part of the book, I share with you both my personal process of reclamation and some snapshots of inspiring client stories. I also include some practices that you can implement to help you integrate these lessons and reclaim your own priestess powers. This work lays the foundation for everything that is to come and it is only when we have given ourselves over to this process that our purpose and strength to live a new way emerges.

THE RETURN OF THE PRIESTESS

A woman undone is a formidable force. As she unravels, the lies and false beliefs that have kept her in bondage begin to dissolve.

She starts to breathe freely and feel fully. Her hair grows wild. Her eyes shine bright. She becomes aware of her sexual magnetism. She starts to honour her intuition. And the flame of her inner power burns brighter. As a result, the portal to the priestess opens.

During my first months living in Portugal, I experienced an awakening like no other. There were intense highs and dark lows as I navigated the process of healing my trauma and recalibrating my being. But despite the storm of emotions that raged through me, I felt grounded. My newly acquired freedom opened me up to the process of self-rediscovery. I no longer had anyone to answer to, no-one to protect myself from, and no-one to justify myself to.

I was free to embody a new identity and, in response, the priestess made herself known to me. I recognised her instantly of course. The embodiment of potent feminine intuition. The vessel of the Divine. The channel of wisdom. The weaver of magic. She started to express herself in the way I dressed, the way I moved, the way I taught my yoga students, the way I talked. And in response to her power, my life started to become magical.

MAURO

I can't believe he's here, sat in front of me. Him. For 29 years I had believed that soulmate love was a thing of make-believe and that when it came to choosing a partner, it was far more sensible to be practical. And look how that turned out. I'd left behind me a trail of lacklustre or downright dangerous relationships. Good job. Yet now I'm in a small traditional Portuguese restaurant talking with the love of my life. It's our first date. But I know. I just know.

I've been living in Portugal for about eight weeks now and I've never felt freer. The despair and loneliness I felt at the beginning simply disappeared one day and was instantaneously replaced with gratitude and wonder. I quickly began to make friends. Long coastal walks, good local wine, heart to hearts and sunset yoga acted like therapy for me and I felt myself returning home. To myself. In fact, I felt powerful and strong in a way that I hadn't for years.

And just a week ago, I had experienced what I can only describe as an activation of the Divine Feminine. I was swimming in the lake with my friend, Reilly, but then suddenly it was like me as the individual no longer existed. Instead, I felt myself merging with the Great Mother. There was divinity in every cell of my being and this feeling lasted for hours. I wondered if I was experiencing a sort of psychosis, but I felt calm and at peace the whole time. And perhaps the most interesting thing is that Reilly was also having a similar experience. We were both sober but drunk on the energy of the Infinite. And during that experience, I was given a clear and life-changing message: your work is women's work and you're here to be a priestess.

The next day I promised myself that I wasn't going to focus on dudes anymore. Ok, maybe I'd allow myself to have a bit of fun, but that was it. Instead, I was going to live my divine mission — to align myself with sisterhood and facilitate women's empowerment. Which is why it's so ironic that, just a week later, I've met him. Him. My mind might be telling me that this wasn't part of the plan. But my inner priestess? She's pouring me another glass of wine and whispering to me to lean in and kiss him.

We cannot live as handmaidens of the Divine whilst we're preoccupied with trying to fix or save a toxic relationship. And paradoxically, until we embrace our personal power, we will continue to be attracted to jerks who do not see us as the powerful women that we are. This is why my relationship with Mauro could only materialise and blossom once I had fully recognised and accepted myself as a powerful priestess.

My relationship with Mauro blossomed and through it I came to understand the true power of the masculine when it isn't blinded by ego. He was, and still is, able to hold incredible space for my feminine creativity, intuition and emotionality. I believe that every woman deserves to be treated with such respect, kindness and reverence. Looking back now, I cannot believe I accepted anything less than this in previous relationships.

It's also no coincidence that uniting with Mauro became a catalyst for an exponential up-level in my life, where I embodied the priestess and channelled her into building a business and creating a life that set my soul on fire. This is what happens when the masculine and feminine fuse together in harmony — magic and exponential growth happen. But more on that later.

ACKNOWLEDGING TRAUMA

I'm eight years old and a Girl Guide (the female version of the Boy Scouts). I'm chatting away to my friends and the next thing I know, our leader, a woman in her thirties we call Brown Owl, starts shouting at me.

'Not everyone wants to know about your posh school, Sarah!'

Stunned, I feel the hot sting of shame reach my cheeks and I bite back my tears.

My parents, wanting the best education for me, had desired to send me to a private school. This wasn't something they could actually afford — my dad was working overtime and I'd been given a scholarship award to reduce the fees.

My Girl Guide friend had innocently asked why my younger brother, Tom, didn't go to the same school and I told her candidly (in the way only a young child can) that my parents didn't have the money. I was already on a partial scholarship. Being called out by Brown Owl in front of all of those kids felt mortifying and the pain of being misunderstood caused me to sob hysterically when my mum came to pick me up. I didn't realise it until I was sat in a session with my therapist as an adult, but my eight-year-old self experienced that fleeting moment as a trauma.

Usually when we think of trauma, we think of Trauma — with a big T — such as abuse, rape, and violence etc. But there's also trauma — with a little t — situations, such as my experience with the Girl Guides, which create a heightened emotional response. In response to the situation, I locked in a belief that I was different and it was dangerous to share my truth. And as a result of this and countless other micro-traumas that I experienced throughout my younger adult years, I found it hard to believe that my opinion was worth anything, and so I stayed quiet.

There are countless circumstances during our lives where we experience these traumas, such as an insult, an offhand comment, or unwanted sexual attention. Men and women both experience trauma. But women's trauma is heavily laced with 3500 years of oppression, persecution and expectation. In response, we have learned to edit ourselves. We carefully choose our words. We avoid expressing our opinions. We avoid wearing skimpy clothing. We avoid following our callings and dreams. We do anything to avoid the possibility of being misunderstood, judged or attacked.

In our culture, it's challenging for women to be fully themselves. We've grown up witnessing the ways in which women in the public eye get slammed for everything they do or don't do. I watched in horror back in 2018 when the brave Christine Blasey Ford testified against the American Supreme Court nominee Brett Kavanaugh. In her testimony, she explained that she felt it was her civic duty to publicly share that Brett Kavanaugh as a teenage boy had assaulted her at a party. I witnessed with disgust how she was taunted and threatened for having the audacity to speak out against him. By many, she was branded a liar. And predictably, Kavanaugh was still sworn in as Supreme Court Judge. I watched him give his own testimony and it made my blood run cold. He was angry, irrational and full of contempt. I couldn't believe that with a performance like this that his nomination would go through. But it turns out he was always President Donald Trump's favourite.

What I saw unfold in this scenario was a textbook case of the patriarchal narrative at play. The story is essentially this: white affluent men are allowed to do what they want without consequence. Women who speak out, however, are made out to be evil.

As you can see, the outside world hardly feels like an encouraging environment for a woman to own her voice and express herself. To the collective feminine, the world feels like an unforgiving and scary place that won't accept her truth. It also won't allow her to speak up, let alone be in process, explore and, yes, mess up from time to time. The only way forward is to heal our individual and collective trauma and choose to muster our own inner courage so that the feminine can truly rise up and reclaim herself. The more of us that speak up and out, the better. I know that we can change this, but we have to be brave, and we have to keep on speaking our truth and being allies to each other.

The trauma that we experience as women is rooted in our ancestry. In the last few millennia, as patriarchy grew in dominance, women's magic and natural healing knowledge was feared. Thousands of women were burned at the stake during the 16th and 17th centuries, and this was after facing torture and humiliation. These witch hunts introduced a system of terror to women. Those who survived this interrogation had to adopt a much more acceptable model of femininity, one where women became obedient and submissive.

New scientific findings have shown that trauma is passed on from generation to generation and researchers have discovered not only can extreme and traumatic events change an individual, but they can also impact their children, generations later.

We store trauma in the body. If we wish to heal our trauma, we must learn to slow down, observe our body and allow it to settle. The experience of feeling unsafe creates physical contraction and, if it isn't released, it becomes crystallised, showing up as tension, pain, or in some cases disease. Emotional trauma imprints the nervous system deeply and quickly. It causes neurological changes in the brain and body which lock us in trauma patterns. Trauma may be reactivated by the slightest provocation, resulting in triggered behaviour. Whilst triggered (also known as flight, fight or freeze), energy is drained from our cognitive centres and vital organs. Therefore trauma can have a huge impact on our decisions, and it is undoubtedly because of trauma that women stay in toxic situations or hold themselves back from shining their brightest light in the world.

The unconscious triggering of the trauma response usually causes us to disassociate from the feelings of non-safety in our body by getting straight into our heads and over-thinking. This is a travesty for the feminine spirit because, whilst she is locked into reliving her trauma response, two of a woman's greatest feminine superpowers are suppressed: her intuition and her creative ability to problem-solve. And it's obvious that we cannot live our fullest expression as priestesses if we are constantly in survival mode.

PRIESTESS POWER

Back into Your Body Sadhana

The word sadhana is Sanskrit and it loosely translates as 'spiritual practice'. Although it's not my heritage, I use the word because it calls to me. When we consistently cultivate our feminine superpowers, we become magnetic.

Use this sadhana daily to cultivate feelings of safety in your body.

Find yourself a space where you won't be disturbed for the next 5 minutes or so and seat yourself in a comfortable upright position, where your spine is straight, your shoulders are released and your face is relaxed.

Close down your eyes and scan your body for sensations. Notice what you notice without judgement and simply witness it.

Start to explore deepening your breath, inhaling through your nose and allowing your belly to fill up during the first half of the inhalation and then drawing that breath up to your heart during the second half. At the top of your inhalation, take a pause, and then slowly let out the breath through an open mouth. Make your exhalations longer in length than your inhalations.Continue to explore this breathing, allowing yourself to release deeper and deeper with each exhalation.

After 5 minutes you can return to your natural breath and scan your body once again. Notice any subtle shifts in energy or sensation.

Finally, take a few moments to wrap your arms around yourself and give yourself a loving hug, as if you're hugging your inner child. Feel your body as the container of all of your experiences and know that right now in this moment, you are safe.

THE TRAUMA OF SOCIAL EXPECTATION

There's an even subtler form of trauma that we face as women. I call it the Trauma of Social Expectation. The list of 'shoulds' that our society has bestowed upon its women is extensive. Each 'should' is like another stick with which to beat ourselves up with. And each of us has collected so many sticks, we could open a museum.

Every woman I have ever worked with has come to me experiencing some form of anxiety, depression, rage, lack of motivation or burnout. All of these are classic symptoms of a woman who's living a way of life that is out of alignment with who she truly is.

Within every woman there's an internal blueprint, made up of our passions, talent, gifts and desires. Like the seed of a wildflower, the blueprint is a code, showing us how we are designed to grow and what we are designed to become. Yet our society despises wild flowers. It calls them weeds and teaches us to pull them up from the earth. And in their place, we are encouraged to cultivate 'more suitable' plants.

But we are wildflowers. This is our nature. And the thing about wildflowers is that you can't control them or suppress them. They are what they are. And they're meant to grow.

For many of us, the external pressure we experience growing up is too much. As a result, our nervous systems go into overdrive to try and keep us safe from rejection. One of the most common trauma responses I witness in the women I work with is perfectionism.

Perfectionism is sneaky because it's so alluring. We want to be perfect, don't we? We want to get everything right first time so that we can please others and avoid the sense of shame that inevitably comes if we fail, or say or do the 'wrong' thing. To the perfectionist, nothing is worse than messing up. We raise the bar so high for ourselves, but then we beat ourselves up for failing to meet our expectations. As a result, we respond in one of two ways: we either procrastinate and put off taking the necessary action to move us closer to our goals, or we overwork, spending endless hours on a project and never feeling like it's good enough. We may, especially for the latter, believe that this is a good thing because it means we're conscientious and responsible. But this is yet another illusion because all we are doing is robbing ourselves of the in the moment joy that can only come when we are focused on the process rather than the outcome.

Perfectionism is the hallmark of 'good girl' conditioning. When we start to recognise how it shows up in our lives and loosen its grip on us, we pave the way for liberation. A woman who is able to dance with her imperfections and let go of the need to get it right all the time is a woman who has disentangled herself from a social narrative that has been keeping women captive for centuries.

The Power of the Priestess — Client Spotlight

Jennifer, a smart and accomplished woman from the USA, with flowing brown hair and golden skin, was no stranger to perfectionism but she had no idea how much it was robbing her of feeling joy. With her focus set on trying to prove herself, she found herself never quite meeting the expectations she had of herself. This meant that she also had high expectations of others, standards that they also could never quite reach. All in all, she felt frustrated with life. Her need to control was getting in the way of her enjoying her life.

As soon as we started working together in one of my group mentoring programmes, she messaged me to tell me that she was already beginning to feel a shift. As the weeks went on, she realised how necessary it was to let go of the expectations she had of herself. This wasn't easy, but she knew it was crucial. Her intention to do this sparked a wave of inner transformation. Not only did she find herself creating more space for herself, she noticed her relationships with others were deepening because she was allowing them to simply be themselves. Loosening up the pressure she'd always put on herself and others allowed her to experience what she had wanted all along — deeper connection and belonging.

RECLAIMING OUR WILDNESS

There comes a moment in every woman's life when she realises that the manual she was handed about what she's supposed to want, who she's supposed to be, and how she's supposed to act, wasn't the right manual for her.

One of two things happens. Either something crumbles — she experiences the loss of a job, a relationship or a family member. Or she experiences a more subtle erosion — she can't quite shake off the feeling that she's not living her truth and each day it eats away at her a little more.

Inevitably, after a while, the search for fulfilment, inner power and real soul-satisfying purpose takes over — it always does. And that's the cue for the priestess to make herself known.

This process doesn't always feel pretty or make sense externally. Sometimes it can look like we're falling apart and often it feels this way too. The people around us will often question us, eager to find a way to 'fix us' during what they perceive to be a breakdown (although we know it's a breakthrough). It's not their fault; they just don't know how to be with their own discomfort, let alone someone else's. And there are others who watch our transformation fearfully and question who we are becoming. If they're used to us being a certain way and derive their sense of self from this, they will often feel threatened by our growth and so they try to cling even tighter to the old version of us. All of this is normal, and yet we must be ready for it and be willing to let go of the people and situations that no longer serve us so that we can continue on our path of reclamation. We must choose the woman we are becoming over the woman we once were, no matter what.

The Power of the Priestess — Client Spotlight

Maria has an incredibly playful and mischievous spirit. In her younger years, she was the life and soul of the party, her long fiery red hair weaving its spell wherever she went. It was hard for men not to fall in love with her. But she'd been trained to be a good Irish Catholic and later found herself under pressure to conform. Even though deep down she knew she shouldn't get married, she did it anyway. The cracks started to appear in the relationship straight away.

Her parents got involved. The in-laws got involved. Endless counselling sessions were scheduled. The social pressure she felt to make her lifeless marriage work was unbearable. But she wasn't yet able to admit it to herself. During our sessions, she slowly began to acknowledge her truth — that deep down she didn't want her to marriage to work because her soul was yearning for more. And once she'd illuminated this, within the space of a few weeks, she'd found the courage to leave him and move to England to take a new job doing what she loved.

Our work together allowed her to realise that there are no such things as 'mistakes' — they are stepping stones to greater clarity about who we are and what we desire. By no longer making herself wrong, she was able to follow what felt right. And now she's living her truth and owning her power.

MEETING YOUR TRUE SELF

The True Self is the blueprint of who you are, what you desire and what you're here to contribute to the world. You are embodying her when you feel expansive, when life feels joyful, when you feel magical and when you're leaning into your growth edges. Living as the True Self doesn't always feel 'good', sometimes it's scary as hell. But it will always make you feel alive. Your True Self is a version of the priestess — if it wasn't, you'd never have been called to pick up this book.

The False Self is the socialised self — the internal rules of behaviour for how we as women should think, look and behave. The conflict between the True Self and the False Self is what keeps us up at night. We worry if we're on the right path, if we've said the right thing, if we're with the right person or if we're settling for what we think we should want or what we think we can get. And it takes up so much of our energy. Which is why when we finally commit ourselves to authentic living, we free up our energy for the things that matter to us.

When we finally decide to commit to our True Self, we are committing to a lifetime of healing, expansion and growth. Contrary to what we've been taught, healing isn't a process that we can tick off our to-do list. It's a process that just keeps on going, bringing us to new depths and new heights.

It takes a truly brave woman to commit to connecting to and honouring her True Self, especially when the social pressure to be the False Self is incredibly strong, which it always is. But it is the only way to live a joyful and liberated life. It is the only way to reclaim our power and reveal our divine purpose. It is the only way to live as the priestess.

Most of our reclamation is about healing our trauma. Not just trauma that happened to us, but the self-betrayal we inflict upon ourselves every time we ignore our inner knowing, beat ourselves up, hate on our bodies or make a decision to please others rather than ourselves.

The portal to priestesshood is to recognise that there's nothing wrong with you. Nothing. Everything you've experienced has been in response to the system of beliefs and ideals that you inherited but didn't ask for.

When you understand this, you can have compassion for yourself, undo this conditioning and become the powerful priestess you're destined to be.

RECLAIMING THE FEMALE FORM

I'm in the back of Abi's mum's car and I've just announced to the pair of them that from now on I'm going to eat only vegetables because I want to lose weight. I'm just 13 years old.

I'm perplexed as to why Abi's mum has such an issue with it. I feel taken aback — surely everyone is trying to lose weight? As she gently tries to explain to me that I need a balanced diet to stay healthy, I zone out to imagine how much better my life will be when I have the perfect figure, the perfect skin and the perfect hair.

We teach our girls to be at war with their bodies before they've even begun to live. As a consequence, I have yet to meet a woman who hasn't at some point in her life thought she was fat, ugly or needed to change something about herself.

De-conditioning from unrealistic beauty ideals is a life-long process. Even today, although in many ways I now accept the way I'm physically put together, I only have to switch on Netflix or scroll on Instagram to be suddenly plunged into the spiral of comparing myself to a feminine ideal that only 4% of the female population naturally fit. More shocking still is the racial bias that exists globally and that black women, indigenous women and women of colour are still hugely underrepresented in the media. When travelling around Asia, it shocked me to see skin-lightening lotions in stores, evidence that the system of white supremacy, as well as patriarchy, is very much etched into the fabric of global society. Speaking to my Filipino friends, I was horrified to learn how much they envied my white skin, believing me to be more beautiful than them because of it. And there was me, lying under the sun as much as I could, desperately trying to obtain the sun-kissed glow that my culture had taught me to strive for.

It affects us all. Although I am white, slim, blonde and young in a society where those traits are celebrated, I've still been taught to disown my physical body. I'm writing this at the age of 32 and there are now subtle lines on my face in places where my skin was once smooth. I desperately want to tell you that I've embraced them but I haven't. The fear began on my 30th birthday. Mauro had bought me a facial and the beautician told me that my skin was ageing too quickly. Yikes.

As a consequence of this offhand comment, I began fixating on my skin and arguing with my reality. I investigated different cosmetic options and I toyed with the idea of injecting all sorts of things into my face. Yet deep down I knew that attempting to resist the natural process of ageing would be out of alignment with what I believe in — and for me, a reclamation of feminine power means fiercely defending my wrinkles.

Because what is Botox, if not yet another way to hate on women? A patriarchal society condemns a woman's wrinkles. A man with silver hair and wrinkles looks 'distinguished' but a woman with wrinkles? She's encouraged to inject poison into her face. How dare a woman be expressive. How dare a woman live a rich and full life. How dare it show on her face. No, we are expected to erase them and look like young girls. Innocent and submissive. Easy to fool and control. Yet if we do inject fillers into our faces, we get judged for it and are encouraged to deny it. Either way, when it comes to our beauty, there's no way we can win.

I'm not easy to fool. So, although I feel the resistance, I, for now at least (who knows later on), choose to keep my wrinkles. I desire to wear them with pride. Because ageing is a privilege. And embracing the wisdom of age is the ultimate rebellion in a society that's desperately trying to infantilise its women.

But there's more to this. When a woman's taught to reject her wrinkles, her cellulite, her tummy rolls, the colour of her skin, she's taught to reject her temple. A woman's body is the temple in which miracles and magic occur. I'm not just talking about the obvious fact that women, should they wish and are able to, can give birth to tiny humans, there's more at play here. A woman who inhabits her body fully is in touch with her own sensuality, her desire, her aliveness, her creativity and her intuition. In essence, she is in touch with her source of feminine power and, of course, it's not surprising that a society rooted in patriarchy finds this unnerving. And this, I believe, is why for millennia and unfortunately even now, women's bodies are made out to be wild, unruly and something to control.

The Pill. Waxing. Bleaching. Diets. Botox. These are all designed to control women's bodies and as a result we learn not to trust them — how could we trust something when we feel the need to control it? But what happens when we do reclaim our trust? Once we start not only loving our body but inhabiting it fully, we reclaim our Divine given superpowers to intuit, create and heal.

INTUITION

For a very long time, I was extremely disconnected from my intuition, having been taught very early on in my life that logic is superior. This led me to make a lot of decisions that took me away from the truth of myself. My relationship with my ex was a prime example of this, but suppressed intuition doesn't just impact upon our love lives. It conditions our day to day decisions, such as what we eat, who we hang out with or what we believe to be true. The quality of our lives isn't just based on our big life decisions. When we're not aligned with our inner guidance system for our day to day choices, life feels calculated, risky and far too serious.

Intuition is the subtle sense of noticing and knowing. It's the ability to understand instinctively without the need for conscious reasoning, and so much of our power as women and as priestesses lies in our intuition. These days, my personal decision-making processes are more aligned than ever before. I've learned that following my intuition's like a VIP Access Pass to exponential healing and growth because, when we connect to our intuitive power, we're able to access the natural laws of magic and co-create with the intelligence of the universe.

The bonus is that it gets to be fun. I enjoy my life more than ever because I'm constantly playing ping pong with the cosmos. The universe pings me an intuitive nudge and then I ping back by taking action. And we play. And we create. And the opportunities and resources I require to live my highest vision always arrive bang on time, even when I doubt it.

Most of us have been taught to use the logic of our mind to make decisions but the mind is often the issue. The mind was designed to dream and vision but it's a terrible decision-maker. If you're trying to make a decision with the mind, it's like navigating new terrain in a blizzard without a map or a compass. Have you ever found yourself going backwards and forwards with a decision, driving yourself insane in the process? That's your mind — fickle and flakey.

The deep calm knowing of intuition lives in our body. Our body gives us physical responses to thoughts, emotions and circumstances. The body can't lie and is an incredible portal to aligned decision making. It can take in everything about a situation and give us a clear and definitive answer about what to do next.

The trouble is most of us are disconnected from our body. The trauma of what it is to be a woman in today's society has made us dissociate and check out from our physical home. The unrealistic social specifications of what a woman should look like has led us to reject our bodies. The critical narratives around a woman's sexuality have made us feel like we're wrong to feel pleasure, and so we don't go there. I sometimes feel like this was a huge plot centuries ago to purposefully shut out feminine intuitive power — Early Christian Church, I'm looking at you! And if it wasn't, it's certainly been a convenient byproduct that's kept the patriarchy in power and the feminine in bondage.

As we reclaim our feminine bodies and learn to listen to its subtle signals, our capacity for intuition increases. The felt sense signature for intuition is different for each of us but it's usually a feeling of expansion or contraction, lightness or heaviness. And the only way we get to know our intuition intimately is to commit to the process of listening.

When my clients start learning to cultivate their intuition, I encourage them to focus their intention on two things. First, I invite them to commit to a practice that allows them to cultivate a connection with their body through mindfulness.

Second, I invite them to create a relationship with their felt sense throughout their daily decisions, including what they eat, where they go and what they choose to wear. This gets to be really fun and playful. And over time, we learn to build self-trust and access our intuitive power for bigger life decisions.

The Power of the Priestess — Client Spotlight

The potency of intuitive work changed everything for my client, Mary. Mary is of Italian descent and has piercing eyes and raven-like hair. She's the priestess incarnate. A doula, her soul mission is to revolutionise how women approach pregnancy, giving birth and motherhood. When she first started working with me, she shared all of this with me, but there was something holding her back. As we dug deeper, she told me she'd been married for 11 years and was happy in her relationship. My inner priestess didn't buy it. She sensed that Mary was living in a cage that she couldn't see.

We got straight to it with the intuition work. Mary had already done an incredible amount of personal development, but she'd been experiencing one stumbling block that so many women face — understanding if her decisions were coming from intuition or fear.

Deep down, she knew that her husband and his family were toxic for her. The red flags were there. The contraction in her belly was there. But like most of us, she was so used to making decisions using logic, she talked herself out of knowing what she knew. As she started doing this deep intuitive work, it all started to unravel and she discovered that she could not embody the priestess, live her purpose and stay in her marriage.

She chose to leave her husband. It was hard. It was painful. But it was liberating. And as soon as she did, within a few weeks, her doula business took off without her even trying. This happened because she had freed herself up to follow her intuitive nudges and let the universe take care of her. Her embodiment of the priestess was so powerful and so transformative that it still gives me the chills. This is the potency of leaning in to our intuitive powers.

IS IT INTUITION OR FEAR?

Have you ever found yourself feeling a strong sense about something but wondering if it's intuition or fear? How do we distinguish between intuition and fear? Intuition as a felt sense is always underpinned by a sense of calm and peace. When we find ourselves in a storm of emotions, we must wait. If there's any emotional turbulence, it's not intuition speaking. If we're doubtful of what to do, we must take a moment to pause, and then do what feels instinctively good — animals always do what feels good, leading them to greater safety. And if we're still not sure if it's intuition or not, we can look to our language, which always gives us away. If we say things like 'I'm trying to figure it out or I'm trying to decide' this is an indicator that we're using logic and not our felt sense intuition.

Sometimes fear-based conditioning will mask itself as intuition, trying to encourage us to stay in our comfort zone. If we feel the panic of fear related to doing something new that initially excited us, it's not our intuition. An intuitive nudge not to do something feels more like a calm inner 'no'.

Many times, we feel the intuitive knowing to get out of a dangerous situation and override it. That contraction in your stomach? Know it. Trust it. Follow it. There are far too many women who have led themselves into danger because they didn't listen to their instincts to run. Whenever we access an intuitive nudge, it's crucial that we follow its wisdom and take action. The more we do this, the more we build self-trust. By making decisions that override our intuitive wisdom we betray ourselves and break our self-trust. This creates the internal blockages that eventually cut us off from our intuition and it becomes a vicious cycle. Therefore, the more we take action on our intuitive guidance, the more we open ourselves to access more of its wisdom.

When it comes to making decisions that go against logic or expectations, we must stay rooted, no matter what. I recently read the phrase 'no is a complete sentence'. I couldn't have put it better myself. We don't need to justify our choices. Ever. We get to choose without explanation. We get to follow our intuition without needing to prove to others that we're right. We get to walk our own path and what we do is no-one else's damn business. This includes friends, partners and loved ones. We owe it to ourselves to be true to our inner guidance system. Because when we become the embodiment of priestess power, it ripples out and gives others permission to honour their true desires and unique path. The strongest energy wins which means we don't need to spend our energy on explaining ourselves or trying to convince others. Instead, by embodying our personal power and being the change we're desiring for the world, we move mountains effortlessly.

Our intuition is innate and it's powerful. Once we are connected to it and we allow ourselves to be guided by it, life flows. Healing happens. And magic and miracles unfold. Because anything is possible when you truly and deeply listen to your inner guidance system.

PRIESTESS POWER

Cultivate Your Intuition Sadhana

Use this exercise to help you explore your intuition. Start with small things, like what to eat or wear, and then build up to bigger choices — this will help you build self-trust.

Think of a situation in your life right now where there is a choice to be made.

List out all the possible choices and responses to this situation.

Go through each one, close your eyes and listen to the response of your body as you imagine the choice.

Notice any decisions that feel heavy, dark or contracting — these are intuitive signals that the choice is NOT in alignment.

Notice any decisions that feel light, expansive, inspiring and freeing — these are signals that this choice IS in alignment.

If all choices feel dark, this is a signal that none of these choices are in alignment — either consider more choices or wait until something else comes up.

Keep a journal of your intuitive journey, making a note of all the sensations that you feel in response to decisions and situations.

RECLAIMING PLEASURE

'What would give you pleasure?' Whenever I ask one of my clients this question, nine times out of ten they will shift with discomfort. As a culture, we know entertainment but we don't know real pleasure. This is even more poignant with Northern European and American culture — in my experience, Latin cultures are more down with experiencing la dolce vita (the sweetness of life).

Pleasure is a portal to infinite healing, creativity and joy. So why is it that we shy away from it? Women have been conditioned to focus on their utility in life over their enjoyment of life. We have been taught that in order to enjoy ourselves, we must first make sure that we've earned it. That to live a life focused only on pleasure is hedonistic, decadent and selfish. That we must forgo what we love in the name of duty and responsibility. And where does all this shame around pleasure really make itself known? In the bedroom.

As you learned in the chapter about the history of patriarchy, women's bodies and their right to feel pleasure have been policed for a long time, particularly when it comes to our sexuality. The idea of pleasure makes us feel uncomfortable because we've been conditioned to believe that it is wrong. And there's nothing that our good girl conditioning hates more than being wrong.

Many women struggle with sex. They often feel shame around their sexual expression. Many of the women I work with have trouble accessing their sexual pleasure. They tell me they are always in their heads during sex. They tell me sex is a painful experience. They tell me they judge themselves for their past 'misconduct'.

The sad fact is that women are statistically more likely to experience burnout. There are a myriad of reasons for this, such as the amount of unpaid work in and out of the home that we're socially expected to do, but really it's because we live in a society that does not allow us to prioritise rest and pleasure.

Pleasure is not only deeply healing for the nervous system (it releases oxytocin, a neurotransmitter responsible for lowering stress), but it's also the biggest rebellion against patriarchal power. Introducing daily pleasure is a way of owning our right to live our lives authentically and to our fullest expression.

I teach all of my clients to cultivate pleasure and sensuality into their daily lives. This can be something as simple as smelling fresh flowers or slowing down to really taste the food you're eating. For many women, when they build their courage, it extends to the art of self-massage and self-pleasure. These practices signal to the nervous system that we're safe and when we have strong feelings of embodied safety, we can move more easily out of the state of survival and bring our focus onto thriving.

When we reclaim pleasure, we reclaim the present moment. We begin to slow down and enjoy the process of life rather than striving for a destination. And invariably, as this happens, we begin to open ourselves up to greater play, creativity and magic.

STOKING YOUR CREATIVE MAGIC

When I was a child I believed wholeheartedly in the existence of magic. And I still do. When I refer to magic, I'm not talking about the supernatural, but the natural forces of creation. Magic is how the universe operates. What's fascinating is that the concept of magic is ancient. In ancient Egypt, magic was seen as the harnessing of natural laws to achieve certain results. To the Egyptians, a world without magic was inconceivable. It was through magic that the world was created and sustained. Magic infused every aspect of ancient Egyptian life — we're talking around about 8000 years ago.

The concept of magic became demonised within Christian belief systems, particularly in relation to women. Magic was seen as dark, supernatural, and of course, we know that many women were persecuted because of this. But magic is simply a word to describe the forces of the universe that allow for humans to create their reality. Vedic (yogic) philosophy acknowledges that pervading all things is an invisible Lifeforce, called Prana (or Shakti), and therefore everything is connected and made of one creative power. This energy is feminine because it is the energy of creation. Women are vessels for creation and our potency for tapping into that universal source of creative energy is infinite.

Creativity and magic go hand in hand — we cannot harness magic without accessing our innate creativity. During my academic years, I researched the nature of creativity as part of my PhD. I discovered that creativity is the lifeblood of any thriving civilization. There's no innovation or exponential growth without it.

Creativity embodies the elements of the mystical. The writer Elizabeth Gilbert sums it up beautifully: 'The magical thinking that I use to engage with creativity is this idea that inspiration does not come from me, it comes to me. And the reason I choose to believe that is because one, that's what it feels like, and two, that's how pretty much every human being before the Age of Enlightenment (in the 1600s) described inspiration.'

The idea that creativity is something that comes through us speaks to the process of co-creation — the process of creating with a higher power. As women and priestesses, we are the Divine vessels through which realities are created and transformed.

Creativity is innate and it's the route to feminine liberation. Our health, sense of well-being, fulfilment and wealth are at their optimum when we engage in creative work that's deeply satisfying to us as individuals and feels spontaneous and playful.

PRIESTESS POWER

Stoke Your Creative Magic Sadhana

Creativity is a magic that you can cultivate. Use these contemplation prompts to uncover and explore what your own playful processes might be:

What fun things would you love to do that would feel too frivolous?

If you didn't have to earn money, look respectable or prove yourself, what would you fill your days doing?

What beliefs, judgements or 'shoulds' get in the way of your creative expression?

In which areas of your life do you feel guilt? What do you need to believe to alleviate this guilt and allow yourself to experience fun?

What activities can you schedule in over the next few weeks that will allow you to honour and cultivate play and creativity in your life?

MOVING PAST THE FEAR OF JUDGEMENT

The fear of judgement is hands down the biggest fear that keeps women captive. If we're not being ourselves fully, sharing our ideas or following our callings, you can bet your last penny that the fear of judgement is getting in the way.

The reason that judgement scares us so much is because, if we let it in, we feel rejected. And we are evolutionally hard-wired to avoid rejection at all costs. Thousands of years ago when we lived in small communities, our survival depended upon our clan or tribe. We needed to be liked. We needed to fit in and be accepted because it was a matter of survival.

In addition to this, for the past four millennia or so, women have had less political and economic power than men. Women's survival was based on keeping the peace, not rocking the boat and playing the part of the good woman. Those who didn't were made an example of.

In this day and age, people's judgement doesn't sign our death warrants but it can still feel like a death to us. Our nervous system doesn't know the difference, which is why it's crucial that we are compassionate with ourselves. At the same time, we must find the courage to no longer let the fear of judgement be in the driving seat of our decisions. Instead, we must grab the fear by the horns and choose to jump on the saddle. This is the only way to heal.

I read a quote once: 'fear is a mask for desire'. In fact, I believe that judgement itself is a mask for desire. We judge in ourselves that which we wish to embrace and we judge in another that which we haven't the courage to acknowledge in ourselves or outwardly express.

The judgements that we fear aren't the monsters that we think they are — they mirror projections, unhealed wounds and secret desires. By believing in the power of judgement as much as we do, we further foster the separation that underpins so much of the darkness in the world. We can choose to change this.

Playing bigger (or truer) and sharing your voice goes hand in hand with experiencing judgement. It's inevitable. You only need to read Amazon reviews of your favourite author to see that this is the case — for every 99 raving reviews, there's always one or two people who didn't like it. People's judgement is simply a reflection of their emotional state, preferences and beliefs. Nothing more.

HEALING THE SISTER WOUND

One of the most traumatic experiences of my life was going to an all girl's school. I went to a Girls' Grammar School from the age of 11-17 (for those of you not in the UK, grammar schools are state schools that pick their students based on academic ability). In theory, this was supposed to be a very nurturing and supportive experience where I'd be given a good education and a head start in life. And yes, I acknowledge how privileged I was to have access to this kind of education, but this doesn't negate the truth: that it was a hotbed of feminine trauma, because, in practice, it was anything but a supportive experience.

Teenage girls can be extremely vicious, especially to those who are different. And I was different. Witchy. Alternative. A rebel. Basically a walking target. And I was mercilessly bullied. Not the 'pull her hair and scratch her eyes out' kind of bullying. I'm talking about the subtle emotionally manipulative tactics that leave a young girl questioning her value and worth and whether anyone can truly be trusted. I wasn't the only one. Girls of different race, body type and economic background were also mercilessly picked on.

Such behaviour is not innate — it's a learned behaviour that occurs in response to a woman's internalised trauma and the deep inner shame of feeling inadequate. I understand now that it was jealousy and insecurity that drove these girls' behaviour to ostracise and ridicule those of us who were different. And I was also no angel. I sometimes joined in with the name-calling in desperate attempts to belong and feel part of something, because let's face it — this is the only reason that we get swept up in such activity.

The Sister Wound — the fundamental mistrust of women by women — is imprinted during our childhood and teenage years but it is created by patriarchy. Patriarchy teaches us to mistrust a woman's power. It teaches us to feel threatened by it. And so, as we reject another woman's essence, we too reject our own inner magic. We simply cannot allow in another woman what we do not allow within ourselves.

Healing the Sister Wound is always a key component of a woman's liberation. Most of the women who join my mentoring programmes have an unconscious mistrust of women. Learning to relax into sisterhood becomes their medicine. And the first point of call is always to question what we have been taught about the way nature works.

We can start with the concept of evolution. Most of us take Darwinian Theory at face value. This is because at school we are taught that evolution is the result of a strategy called 'survival of the fittest'. We are taught that animals are in competition with each other and only the dominant survive. Yet we only have to look at nature to recognise that this isn't necessarily the case. Gaia Theory sees planet Earth as a living system and treats humans as a seamless continuum of that system. It was developed in the late 1960s by Dr. James Lovelock, a British scientist and inventor. The Gaia Paradigm uses the powerful metaphor of 'Gaia' to take into account that we are part of a living system. The theory argues that living organisms and their inorganic surroundings have evolved together as a single living system. The patriarchal paradigm flies in the face of this, making us believe that dominance and hierarchy are the rules by which the world operates. But I believe we should question this and look at life through the lens of collaboration.

Women are collaborative by nature. We know this intrinsically. And when women gather together, magic is created and realities transform. The truth is that we are not in competition with each other, no matter how much our cultures and societies have tried to make us believe that we are. Competition isn't necessary for survival. And if we want to thrive as a species and as a planet, collaboration is what's necessary.

How do we know that we're operating from the Sister Wound? Take a moment to contemplate a woman who you secretly (or not so secretly) condemn or judge. Perhaps it's her success, her failure or the way she carries herself, but there's something about her that you reject. Why is that? Do you see yourself in her? Is she living her life in a way that secretly you wish to?

Another way to know if we're operating from the Sister Wound is to notice where we're avoiding shining too brightly, whether it's sharing our celebrations, making more money, or putting ourselves down when people congratulate us for our efforts or achievements.

Most of the women who join my group mentoring programmes are familiar with the Sister Wound. Initially, they feel resistance to sharing their doubts, fears and processes vulnerably with the group, but eventually, the walls of defence crumble. They learn that sharing their truth is not just medicine for them as individuals but it's also for the collective feminine. There is an incredible amount of power in sharing our most shameful secrets with women who have earned the right to hear them. There is even more potency in hearing them respond to us with the words 'me too'. When I first started facilitating women's work in groups, I totally underestimated the transformative power of sisterhood. Now, it's a crucial element of the work that I facilitate. All of us deserve to be seen, heard and understood fully, and without judgement.

When we take steps to heal the Sister Wound, we're able to further step into our feminine power and two things happen as a result. First, we understand that we are all the same even if we are different. Our struggles, fears and doubts are so much more collective than we realise and in recognising this, we free ourselves up from the worry that it's only us. Second, we learn that by shining brightly, we don't dim the light of others. Instead, we help illuminate their way.

WHY FEMININE POWER IS FEARED

I'm 31 and I'm sat cross-legged on my therapist's comforting couch. Strangely the tears aren't flowing as I share my heart with her, but maybe that's because my eyes are now as dry as the Sahara. I've been crying for three weeks straight and she's been helping me unravel the origins of a deep grief that's been pouring out of me recently. I'm feeling unbelievably vulnerable and raw.

The reason I'm there is that a few weeks ago a friend suddenly stopped replying to my messages. We'd formed our friendship quickly and deeply. We'd helped each other a lot. And I loved her dearly. I felt so sparkly with her and I relaxed into our friendship, believing I could be myself around her.

But for the past few weeks? Radio silence. The story that has kept circling around my mind is the one I've always tried so hard to ignore. But now it's here, screaming at me, and the shame I feel in my body feels almost too much to bear.

You're too much for people, Sarah.

In the past couple of years, I'd come to embody my authentic self and I'd learned that she was pretty powerful. And yet, deep inside of me, this up-levelling was accompanied by fear and resistance. On one hand, I crave expansion above anything else. But on the other hand, I don't want my growth to make anyone feel inferior. I don't want anyone to think I'm too big for my britches. I don't want my growth to make anyone feel uncomfortable.

In the wake of her silence, I began torturing myself. I made myself wrong. I beat myself up for shining too bright. For wanting too much. For being too much. All I wanted to do was hide under the bedcovers and sleep forever. It was all too much. I eventually learned the reason why my friend had pulled away so quickly — to take space from the friendship because she felt that there was a power dynamic between us. When I heard this, the shame spiral began and I went to pieces. Again. A deep inner wound had been gouged open. And so here I am, sat with my therapist, trying to glue the pieces of my broken heart back together.

My breakthrough happened a few weeks after I'd finished my therapy sessions — the bodily trauma began to unravel and release. I suddenly realised that my friend's decision to cut me out was never a true reflection of me, as I had initially believed, but instead reflective of the deep pain she was feeling inside of herself.

I learned that we only reject the power in others when we reject our own power. And real feminine power doesn't subscribe to the traditional patriarchal approach to power. In a patriarchal paradigm, power is seen as something to wield over another. We must be Top Dog. True feminine power is non-hierarchical. It's a recognition of the power within each and every single one of us and an acknowledgment that we truly are all one. And on top of this, there's a recognition that we are always in process. In embodying this truth, we're able to lean back to empower others. We're able to lean in to discomfort to truly listen to others. We're able to simultaneously teach and learn.

EMBRACING EMOTIONALITY

When I was deep in the process of grief after the unexpected death of my brother Nev, I learned some peculiar things about people. There were some friends who didn't know what to say to me and so they ignored me. And there were others who worried incessantly about me, frightened that I couldn't seem to pull myself together.

In response to the grieving process, my habits changed. Rather than spending Friday evenings in the pub (a standard British tradition), I was going to evening kirtan to sing devotional songs in Sanskrit. This perplexed and worried my friends who were convinced that I was joining a cult. But I was being very intentional. I needed to make sense of my pain and the only way I could do that was to feel it and offer it up to the Divine, rather than numb it with alcohol.

Being with deep emotional pain is simultaneously our biggest challenge and greatest liberator in modern times. It's not unusual for the women who work with me to initially deny or judge their heavy emotions — they desperately try to push away anxiety, depression or anger whenever it comes knocking. And it's no surprise — since our early childhood years, society has given us the message that these emotions are bad and that if they come visiting, there must be something wrong with us.

Our everyday speech gives it away. How many times have you been asked how you are and answered it with a simple 'fine, thank you'? But perhaps the truth was that you were not 'fine' — you were tired, anxious, or pissed off... Or perhaps you were feeling incredible and joyous. And the 'fine, thank you' automation downplayed your utter rapture and ecstasy.

Many women on their spiritual path learn that emotions come

through us and that we are not our emotions. And yet the cultural conditioning is so strong that we still try to bypass anything that feels heavy or unfavourable. Or we judge what we are feeling. When jealousy comes to visit, instead of feeling it with curiosity, we feel guilty or ashamed. This creates a compound effect where we experience layers of heavy emotions that we're unwilling or perhaps unable to feel and release.

A woman who rejects her emotional experience rejects a huge part of herself. We cannot accept ourselves fully if we deny or suppress our right to messy expression. What happens when a woman learns how to accept her emotional world fully and to feel, express and release the emotions as they come through? She is no longer a slave to them. She no longer has to spend vast amounts of energy trying to keep them in check. Instead, they become messengers to her, letting her know when her thoughts, actions or environment are in or out of alignment. What I learned during my grieving process was potent and life-changing. Not only did I learn how to feel, I also learned that, as human beings, we can truly handle any emotion.

The word emotion comes from the word emote which means 'to move out'. Emotions are designed to be felt and released. The issue is that we've been conditioned to suppress and repress them. Any emotion that is not fully honoured is stuffed down into the recesses of the body. This creates physical and mental tension that gets triggered and activated by the slightest provocation. It's why we can overreact and lash out uncontrollably at the slightest thing or unexpectedly burst into tears of exhaustion and overwhelm. Like an animal that's been injured, we stumble around, the wounds of our emotional trauma splitting open at the slightest touch. Without giving ourselves the permission to tend to the emotional wounding that we're so desperately trying to avoid, we never heal. And these wounds impact almost every area of our lives.

We've been led to believe that we are rational and logical beings, or at least we should be. But this isn't true. We are emotional in nature and every single decision we make is underpinned by our emotional state at the time. Every single one.

When we are feeling happy or excited, we make decisions that are in alignment with our highest good. When we are feeling scared, our anxieties lead us to make decisions that may bring relief in the short-term but rarely allow us to become the empowered and free women we're destined to be.

In the relationship with my ex, my emotions led to me making some extremely questionable choices when it came to my happiness and my safety. I feared that I wasn't enough. I feared to be by myself. I feared that I couldn't handle the pain of a break-up. This fear led me to put up with verbal and physical abuse that no-one should be subjected to. In the short-term, the decision to stay with him brought me short-term benefits — I didn't have to face the temporary pain of leaving, having to fend for myself and figure out my living situation and my finances. And as humans, we are hard-wired to avoid pain at all costs. To my mind, the pain of leaving outweighed the pain of staying, until the scales were tipped and it became more painful to remain than to go.

Pain can actually be our greatest liberator. That's not to say that we need pain for our liberation — I see many women who are addicted to pain, unconsciously playing the role of martyr and keeping themselves stuck and small in the process. But when we do experience pain, if we are brave enough to give ourselves over to its teachings, we can begin to develop an understanding of our purpose here on earth.

When we embrace our emotions, listen to their wisdom, and allow them to move through us as they were intended to, we build emotional resilience. This built-in ability to respond to stressful situations with focus and grace allows us to stay in our lane and continue in the direction of our dharma. Without it, setbacks become roadblocks, inhibiting our every move and keeping us stuck.

We spend the vast majority of our lives trying to avoid pain, believing that we can outwit it, because we've been taught that pain is weakness and courage can exist without it. But this is a false and damaging narrative. Courage and vulnerability go hand in hand. The most courageous women I have ever met have the capacity to put themselves into situations that will trigger their pain but liberate their souls. Growth is uncomfortable. Following our life's mission can be equal parts exhilarating and painful. But we cannot live full lives without fully dedicating ourselves to the experience of the full spectrum of human emotions and moving past the very emotional trauma that is keeping us chained so tightly.

Emotional pain has a bad reputation in our global society. But it's our greatest ally on the journey of expansion and awakening. I have also noticed that not all pain is the same. There is the pain of discomfort and growth. This happens when we put ourselves out there by speaking our truth or asking for what we desire. And as we feel it we heal it and transcend, bit by bit. But there is also the pain of being unconsciously stuck in damaging cycles that we keep contributing too and are not aware enough to move out of. In a similar way to being caught in a rip current, the more we struggle and fight, the more we exhaust ourselves into oblivion.

So how do we navigate our emotions, heal our trauma and build emotional resilience? We stop trying to get anywhere. We tune into our body. We learn how to feel every single sensation, emotional signature, thought and belief. We recognise that our body is the container of all of our experiences. We feel into it.

We breathe. We stretch and move and wiggle it out. We express. We give ourselves over to our present experience and we allow it to move through us, breath by breath, stretch by stretch, tear by tear, groan by groan.

This is why emotional release and resilience are at the foundation of everything I teach the women I work with. And in many ways, this is the work of the priestess — emotional alchemy. When we give space for ourselves and others to honour their experience but not get stuck there, we facilitate great healing and expansion for all.

The Power of the Priestess — Client Spotlight

Three months into working with me, Jenny and I were on a one-to-one call and she looked completely dejected. When I probed her about what was going on, she replied with: 'Even though we're doing all of this empowering work together, I'm still having days when I feel anxious or sad and I keep thinking there must be something wrong with me. I'm doing everything I can to avoid falling apart completely.' I smiled, knowing exactly what was happening because I'd seen it so many times before — she was making her emotions wrong. She was judging herself for experiencing 'bad' emotions and as a consequence, she believed that she wasn't making progress. Not only that, by trying so desperately to keep things from falling apart, she wasn't allowing Life to do its job. The truth is that sometimes things really do have to fall apart and it's only through death and destruction that situations can regenerate themselves and we can be reborn.

During our session, I challenged her to explore two things. First, I invited her to become curious about her emotions, rather than judging them. And second, I challenged her to let things fall apart, knowing full well that if she allowed herself to let go of needing to control her experience so tightly, this would be the last thing that happened. She took these suggestions in her stride. And of course, nothing fell apart. In fact, it fell together.

Jenny's breakthrough happened when she gave herself permission to 'simply be'. To this day, she's still in the process of allowing herself to feel what she's experiencing and let go of trying so hard to control her experience of life. It's daily sadhana. But at the time of writing this, she's experiencing more relief and presence than ever before.

ILLUMINATE & TRANSCEND
End of Chapter Contemplations

Contemplation is the process of bringing something into our awareness and allowing the light of our consciousness to reveal the layers of its meaning to us time and time again. It encourages true transformation by providing space for us to gain deeper clarity on our insights and integrate them into our lives.

You can contemplate through journalling or by going for a walk in nature and asking yourself the question over and over again.

Don't rush through this process. Give yourself space and time for the wisdom to emerge and you'll be blown away by what you discover.

Here are the contemplative prompts for this chapter:

- What resonated with you throughout these pages?

- What have been your biggest breakthrough realisations so far?

- How can you integrate these realisations into your life?

REVELATION

Embodying the priestess is about reclaiming our feminine power. It's also about tapping into magic and bringing in opportunities and resources that allow us to follow our callings and live our purpose. And finally, it's about helping others heal and self-actualise. The more people that come to transcend their limitations and know who they really are, the more balanced and fair our world will be. Our role as priestesses is to be the channels through which this can take place.

The process of revelation is the point at which we begin to acknowledge and own our skills, our talents and our gifts. It's also where we make the brave decision to begin channelling them into something tangible. As this happens, we become clearer on what we're here for and what we're no longer available for. During this part of the book, I share with you my personal process of revelation where I came to know the priestess. As I began to fully own my priestesshood, I gained clarity on my purpose. In this section, I also offer you some powerful reflective practices to help you do the same.

THE WAY OF THE PRIESTESS

Throughout this book so far, you've heard a lot about my story and how the priestess had been calling to me throughout my life. Now it's time to meet her and begin the process of embodying her so that you too can awaken your feminine power and walk hand in hand with the Divine. Throughout these explorations of who she is and what she represents, I invite you to feel into your body and experience her not just as a concept, but as a living energy within you. To fully welcome her in, we must not only understand her intellectually, but experience her through the loving lens of our heart.

Who is she? And why is she calling to you? Throughout human history — in fairy tales, folklore, literature and film — we find universal characters. These are what the psychologist, Carl Jung, in the 1900s, called archetypes. They're responsible for unlearned, instinctive patterns of behaviour that are burrowed within the psyche of the individual and are simultaneously embedded within the collective unconscious. The seven most common feminine archetypes for Jungian psychologists are the mother, the maiden, the queen, the huntress, the wise woman, the mystic, and the lover. Yet the truth is that we have access to an infinite number of archetypes within us, far beyond the scope of these seven. These energetic blueprints represent inner forces that impact upon who we are being and therefore how we show up in the world, the actions we take and the decisions we make.

As individuals, we tend to have a natural inclination towards embodying the energy of certain archetypes over others. This is shaped by our unique nature, the environment in which we were raised in and live, and what we believe. And then there are other archetypes that are buried in our subconscious, suppressed under layers of social and cultural conditioning.

Within the psyche of every woman is the blueprint of the priestess. She's the vessel of the Divine, channelling divine wisdom and power to serve and facilitate transformation. She's the weaver of magic. When we feel the call to break with convention and live life on our terms, that's her. When we feel the pull to teach, or facilitate, or express, or speak, or create, or be an activist, it's her. We are now living at a precipice where the feminine is rising; the way we having been operating the world is being called to change and we, as priestesses, are part of this shift. This is undoubtedly the reason why you picked up this book — because you are destined to play a part in the Great Uprising.

The Priestess is the embodiment of mystery, alchemy and transformation. She's able to cut through the illusion of disempowerment and tap into the power of potential and possibility. Her role is that of the visionary and the creator of sacred space. Her superpowers are intuition and bold truth. She's an action taker, able to place ego to the side and do what is necessary for the liberation of all. She is rooted, yet soft. Compassionate, yet takes no bullshit.

Embodying the priestess is about reclaiming our feminine power. It's also about tapping into magic and bringing in opportunities and resources that allow us to live our purpose. And finally, it's about helping others heal and self-actualise. The more people come to transcend their limitations and know who they really are, the more balanced and fair our world will be. Our role as priestesses is to be the channels through which this can take place.

PRIESTESS POWER

Activating the Priestess Sadhana

There's a reason that you felt called to read this book — the priestess has been calling to you. It's time to activate her and acknowledge her presence within you.

Use these contemplative prompts to explore:

Who is the priestess to you? How do you sense her energy? What does she symbolise?

In which ways has the priestess been calling to you?

What message does she have for you? What's she trying to tell you?

In which ways do you imagine channelling her wisdom? Through writing, speaking, teaching etc?

THE POWER OF CO-CREATION

When I first moved to Portugal, I had £200 in my bank account, few work prospects and nowhere to stay long-term. As soon as I arrived I was told it would be challenging to not only find somewhere to live over the summer but also to find steady yoga teaching. I didn't take too much heed of this advice. I chose to believe that I'd be taken care of and, because of this unshakeable sense of certainty, I paved the way for magic and miracles to unfold.

Aljezur seemed to me to have an energy of its own and I somehow felt that it wanted me there. I had no work but by chance, I met a guy who turned out to be the manager of a yoga retreat space. He mentioned that they desperately needed a teacher for the entire season and, within two days, I was teaching, embodying the priestess once more. I was without a car but whenever I needed a ride all I had to do was start walking and someone always stopped to pick me up. I was without a place to stay but somehow housesits and short-term rentals came my way just as I needed them. And of course, I also met Mauro. This is the way the universe works. When we believe we will be taken care of, this is what we experience.

There's a natural intelligence that permeates all things in the universe. Everything is connected and forms part of a greater whole. I like to call this 'Cosmic Entanglement'. A powerful example of this lives within our bodies. Our hearts beat because we need to move the molecule haemoglobin around. Haemoglobin carries a smaller molecule, Heme-Fe, and at the centre of that is a single atom of iron. Iron is an element that binds with oxygen and it's this that allows us to move life-nourishing oxygen throughout our circulatory system. Here's the magic: the only way iron is created in the universe is through supernovas and supermassive black stars. These form when galaxies collide. And so, as you read this, I invite you to feel into the beat of your own heart and recognise that those iron molecules dancing throughout your body, keeping you alive, once existed in outer space. As individuals we're not separate from the universe — science and spirituality show that we're part of her.

The idea that we're separate from the cosmos, nature and each other is humanity's biggest illusion. All things are connected and therefore how we feel and what we do truly matters. Not only do we impact upon the field of reality but we're integral to reality itself. Through our connection to all things, we're able to initiate great change. The things that we see as external are actually part of us. We all have the power to consciously create our reality and as priestesses not only do we know this, but we embody it.

The mind has a direct impact upon our creation of reality but it also plays a huge part in our perception of it. Reality is radically different depending on whom you talk to. There are people who live well into their hundreds who never get cancer. There are others who eat all the junk food under the sun and never put on weight. Emile Coué, a French psychologist born in the 19th century, discovered what we now call the 'placebo effect'. He noticed that when he really emphasised a medicine's healing benefits, his patients got better. In fact, Coué stated that 93% of his patients saw dramatic improvement when he raved about how marvellous the medicine was. When he said nothing, the effects of the medicine were less dramatic. Coué knew it was the power of the subconscious mind that healed his patients.

Our belief structures create our perception and interpretation of reality. We actually don't see life as it really is, we see life through a lens. This is because our brains literally could not process all the sensory information that is around us, and to cope, we filter it through our belief system. As a result, we search for evidence that confirms what we believe to be true — we literally interpret, favour and recall information that confirms our pre-existing beliefs. Now that's not to say that social injustices and the inequality we see in the world are the fault of the oppressed. That's really not true. But oppressive social systems such as patriarchy, racism and discrimination are held firmly in place by toxic belief structures. I'll speak more about this later. Our job as priestesses is to change what we believe to be true about ourselves and what we're capable of so that we show up differently and facilitate the global healing, growth and expansion that we're here to.

All creation is co-creation. We co-create with what already exists, be it materials, knowledge or each other. We are also engaging with the source of creation itself. We can call this God, Goddess, The Divine, The Universe, or Source. It doesn't matter what we call it — it's the invisible intelligence that runs through all things. It's the same intelligence that's beating our hearts, regulating our hormones and pumping our lungs.

Co-creation is an underpinning driver of evolution and is an impulse of the universe that can't be controlled by humans. Socially and spiritually, we're evolving at an accelerated rate. We only have to look back upon thousands of years of history to understand this. Before the Neolithic in Europe (roughly 6000 years ago), humans were simple hunter-gatherers, meaning that they hunted for meat and foraged for vegetation. During the Neolithic, the practice of agriculture emerged. Soon after came the Bronze Age, around 4500 years ago, which is when metalworking, a technology that hadn't previously existed, was invented. This allowed for a huge increase in innovation and people made objects that they had never made before, such as metal swords and jewellery.

For the next 4300 years, technological evolution was relatively incremental. But then came the Industrial Revolution, taking place nearly two centuries ago. From that point onwards, there's been an influx in technological advancement leading to a rapid rate of social evolution. With the invention of the internet, access to powerful and sacred knowledge has become more readily available and, as a consequence, we're spiritually evolving more than ever before.

There's an incredible force pulling us forward, elevating our understanding, evolution and consciousness at an accelerated rate. Jean Houston, a founder of the human potential movement, calls this 'entelechy' — the pull of the future towards its manifestation of higher consciousness. In essence, the Divine is pulling us toward her, begging us to meet her. Human beings want to know who they truly are. And as priestesses, we are integral to this process. We are the conduits between earth and sky, planet and Source. We are the midwives to the elevation of consciousness.

Our deepest desires are the medium through which the Divine communicates to us during this process. By honouring our desires and callings, we come to know our dharma — our purpose in this lifetime. In order for us to live to our callings with the path of least resistance, we must be open to see the signposts of the universe and take action. This requires that we be an open channel and find the courage to discover and live our true purpose.

FOLLOWING YOUR CALLINGS & LIVING YOUR DHARMA

Every woman experiences callings within her lifetime — a sense of what she's here to do and what she desires to experience in the world. Callings can be big or small but they are almost always filled with a sense of wanting to make the world a better place. You might find yourself feeling called to work with children, or animals, or to write, or paint, or share your story, or teach, or grow vegetables, or do something for your community. These callings are signposts from the universe, pointing you towards your dharma. Very often though, we ignore them, choosing instead to do what we feel we're 'supposed' to.

I first came across the concept of dharma when I was studying with my spiritual teacher, Satyananda. It's both a Hindu and Buddhist concept related to the fulfilment of our personal duty. An example of dharma is offering a thirsty person a drink because it's an action that's in alignment with our highest nature. Nowadays in spiritual discourse, the concept of dharma is bound up with the idea of purpose.

My experience and personal understanding of dharma is that it's inextricably linked to priestesshood. Priestesshood is the collective dharma of the feminine, but within that, we all have our individual dharma. We're here to play the roles that only we can play and contribute to the healing and evolution of the planet in our own unique way.

Each of us is here to channel the priestess differently, and this depends on our skills, experience, talents and desires. We're all here to facilitate the healing and evolution of the planet but we're not here to do it in the exact same way.

For some of us, our individual dharma is to create beauty. For others, it's to speak truth. And for others still, it's to inspire or hold space. Stepping into priestesshood isn't prescriptive and there isn't a 'right' way to do it. Instead, it's about deeply listening to what we're being called to do, and honouring the path that the cosmos presents to us, no matter how illogical or scary it feels.

I know without a shadow of a doubt that deep down you have a feeling that you know what your purpose is. Perhaps you get inspired by what others are up to in the world. Or maybe even jealous. These are your clues. Especially if you believe that someone like you couldn't do something like that — this is how you know you're onto something. Personally, I knew that living my priestesshood lay in facilitating women's growth long before I finally found the courage to unapologetically own it and commit to it. I knew this because I felt jealous of others who were doing it. And I kept telling myself that I didn't know how.

Priestesshood and following our callings go hand in hand with bravery because it means embracing a completely different way of being. It means going against what society has told us we should do or be. It means stepping into our Divine Feminine power. It means moving past our fear of inadequacy and the lies that we constantly tell ourselves about who we are and what we're capable of. It's about learning how to trust ourselves. And it means trusting Life to provide for us and show us the way.

LIFE IS YOUR PHD

There's no doubt about it: if you're reading this, you're a priestess. And I'd like to bet that, just like I did, you've been hearing her call throughout your life. If you've been looking for a sign, this is it. It's time to find the courage and clarity to fully own who you're here to be and what you're here to contribute. Every life experience up until now has come into your life to prepare you for your role of priestess and you've already done so much of your training without even realising it. In my case, I'd been apprenticing with her for years, I just hadn't been aware of it.

My priestesshood revealed itself to me bit by bit. A few years into teaching yoga, I started to have the feeling that perhaps I could be facilitating women's transformation in a deeper way, as an intuitive guide. I had a deep desire to work with women one-to-one or in small groups online but I was terrified because I felt like an imposter. The voice of doubt was strong. I found myself asking questions that continued to spike my anxiety and stop me from taking action. 'Who am I to guide other women? Don't I need qualifications to prove I'm good enough? What if people judge me? What if they think I'm a fraud? What if I don't know enough?'

I didn't recognise it straight away but this kind of self-doubt is the hallmark of patriarchal conditioning. From an early age, we are taught that in order to be good enough, we need something outside of ourselves. We need the grades and the qualifications. We need the approval of others. And even when we do get the piece of paper, we still find excuses to hold back from shining.

On reflection, no piece of paper has ever given me the confidence that I thought it would. When I graduated from my yoga teacher training, despite having been given the piece of paper, I still felt like I didn't know what I was doing and it took me months to get started. When I graduated from my PhD, I told myself that there must have been a mistake or that perhaps they let me pass because they were being kind. No qualification has ever made me feel better about myself and my capabilities. Ever.

It took me years to understand that life is our PhD. This means that life gives us situations and experiences to navigate and transcend and, in that process, we learn more than we ever could by sitting in a classroom. As priestesses, each of us has unique medicine and codes of transformation that we're here to offer the world. They have been gifted to us throughout our experience of life. Everything we need to do the work we know deep down we're here to offer is inside of us, waiting to be acknowledged. And what needs refining and honing will happen over time as we engage with our craft and learn and refine new skillsets.

I already had everything I needed within me to start facilitating transformative work with one-to-one clients and groups because life had been training me for years. During my university days, I worked as a part-time shop assistant for a New Age store. Year after year in that role, I learned not only powerful transformative practices, but also how to provide comfort and insight for those in need of it. I had also been practicing and sharing the wisdom of yoga for years. The truth was that I was already facilitating transformation for others — I just wasn't owning it.

Stepping into priestesshood isn't about waiting until an authority figure tells us we can do it. It's about reclaiming our Divine-given right to facilitate the work we know deep down we're here to do. It's about fully owning the innate gifts that we use every day and honing our craft day after day. It's about unapologetically sharing them with the world. It's about choosing to step into our role of divine leadership with determination and courage. It's about exploring and big leaps of action towards what's calling us, trusting that we will learn what we need to and be shown the way.

You already have what it takes to move towards what's calling you. You already know enough to begin, more than enough in fact. You are already qualified enough to get started. Why? Because the Divine doesn't give us a desire without also gifting us with the inner resources to get started with it. And yes, it may feel aligned to go deeper and get additional training, some of our callings require this of us, but this is only empowering to our priestesshood when it comes from desire and curiosity, rather than the fear that we're not good enough as we are. If you feel called to work with animals, but you believe the only way to do this is to go to veterinary school for many years (and that's not an option for you), you're missing the point. There are countless ways you can honour this calling, for example, by volunteering or offering your services as a pet-sitter. If you feel called to help women heal their inner wounds, but you believe the only way to do that is to do a psychology degree, again you're missing the point. You could instead start teaching what you've learned about feminine empowerment or ecology or spirituality by starting a podcast or social media account. There are millions of ways to honour your callings, some of which require degrees and some of which do not. Understanding this means that you have no excuse — other than your fear — not to follow what's calling you. Not every calling we have requires that we turn it into a business, movement or non-profit, but every calling needs to be honoured, otherwise we end up dying with our magic still inside of us.

We're not channelling our priestesshood when we're making a plan of what we're going to do. Not even close. Living an empowered life means making empowered decisions. The more leaps into the unknown that you can take, the better. I'm not saying the net will always catch you. Sometimes it won't.

Sometimes you'll leap, you'll fall down, and you'll break something. But as you tend to what's broken and it starts to mend, you'll find yourself surrounded by medicine, the very medicine that will bring you closer to becoming the woman that you're supposed to be. When we commit to taking action before we feel ready, we open the doorway for the priestess to walk through and reclaim herself.

PRIESTESS POWER

Connecting to your Dharma Sadhana

I believe that you already know your dharma but it may be buried under layers of fear and social obligation.

Use these contemplative prompts to explore your soul's calling and purpose:

What do you desire for your life and for the planet?

What is something you see yourself doing in the future that you don't feel ready for now?

What do you see others doing that you wish you could do?

What comes effortlessly to you?

What do you love to do?

What have you overcome in your life and what did you learn?

What are you obsessed about?

What are the stories that you're telling yourself that are stopping you from honouring your desires and callings?

What's the evidence that you have that these stories are made up?

How can you honour these desires often?

PACHAMAMA

I'm 27 years old and stood at the Peruvian-Bolivian border, saying goodbye to a Bolivian tour guide that I've known for three days. I'm desperately trying not to cry. It doesn't make any logical sense because we barely know each other. And I have no idea how he feels about me because we've been nothing but professional with each other over the past days. What I do know is that my heart has chosen him. And now he's walking away from me.

If I had been travelling by myself, I would have followed him, but the thing is that I'm actually working. South America and Peru in particular have always called to me. So, when the opportunity came up within the company I'm working for to manage a three-week archaeology tour there, I went for it. I lied to my boss about my proficiency in the Spanish language (which was dire then and even worse now) and a few weeks later I'd landed in Lima with a group of British geriatrics who were there to learn the Incas and Andean culture.

As soon as my feet touched Peruvian soil, and I heard one of my first (of what would be many) flute renditions of El Condor Pasa, I felt a strange sense of belonging. And as we began our journey down the Peruvian coast and then across the Andes to Bolivia, I began to feel Pachamama's arms embracing me. Pachamama is the Incan earth goddess, revered by indigenous people of the Andes. And she's still very much alive there — you can see offerings to her scattered all across the landscape — which is why I felt incredibly connected to her.

A couple of weeks into our tour, we hopped over the border into Bolivia to stay at the edge of Lake Titicaca and visit the Islands of the Sun and the Moon. Eduardo was the group's guide. He was helpful and kind — I liked him immediately. We got on incredibly well and chatted about all things: nature, politics, religion and philosophy. On our last day together, as we were heading to cross the border back to Peru, it hit me like a freight train out of nowhere.

I love this man.

What the hell? Really? I mean, I didn't even know him and he certainly hadn't given me any indication that he felt the same. It didn't make any sense. But as our tour group was approaching border control, Eduardo turned to me and placed something in my hand. As I looked down I saw that it was his Andean cross necklace — he'd previously told me that he'd had it for years and never taken it off. I placed it around my own neck and suddenly understood that, for whatever reason, this man was going to be an important person in my life.

As I stood at the Peruvian-Bolivian border, I tried very hard to keep myself together as I watched him turn and fade from view. I told myself that the feelings I had for him would be my own little secret.

I had 10 more days left in Peru with my group but my mind was elsewhere. Perhaps it showed — I remember one of the older ladies from the group giving me a knowing wink when she mentioned Eduardo's name. Throughout that time, Eduardo and I started messaging each other back and forth. Within a few messages, he'd admitted to me that he felt the same way and within a few days we were planning how I could come back to Bolivia to be with him.

I remember feeling so certain that this was the sign from the universe I'd been waiting for. The universe was calling me to make a move and follow my heart. Looking back now, this was also an opportunity for escape. During this time, not only was I living in 9-5 hell, but I was also in a relationship with the soon-to-be batterer. It had already turned emotionally abusive at this stage, but I wasn't yet fully aware of it and I had no idea how bad it would end up being.

On returning to the UK, Eduardo and I called each other nearly every day in secret, planning and plotting my return. I had arranged to work at an eco-farm just outside of La Paz. I hid everything from my partner. Fearful even then to invoke his anger, I was biding my time, waiting to tell him that I was leaving and why.

He suspected, of course, and one day, on the way back from work, I received a message from him.

'You're dead to me.'

I knew instantly what had happened — he'd obviously found my journal and read it. I'd spilled my heart onto those pages, weighing up my decision and trying to make sense of the deep knowing that was in my soul. I spent the rest of my journey home in a blind panic, wondering what I would be coming home to. As I opened the front door, the entire house was pitch black. I was scared as I walked through the house, wondering what I would find. He was sat on the stairs, quiet. I expected him to be angry. I had anticipated that most of my stuff would be destroyed. But he was just sat there, motionless. We talked. I explained. And he pleaded with me. He told me he'd be a better partner. He told me all the things I wanted to hear. And then he gave me an ultimatum: him or Eduardo. I chose him.

To this day, I wonder what would have happened if I'd been brave enough to follow my heart. But I wasn't. Fear was keeping me prisoner in this relationship and was seducing me into believing that he would change. He made me cut Eduardo out and block him on social media. And for the next couple of months, we were 'happy' — he was attentive and loving in a way he hadn't been since the beginning. But no matter how much I'd tried to convince myself, there was still part of me that knew I'd copped out of following what my soul was telling me to do.

Perhaps reading this has brought up memories of times in your own life where you've ignored the calling of your soul and opted to 'play it safe'. And somehow, you're either convincing yourself of why you had to make that choice or berating yourself for not being braver. Whatever you've chosen in your past, know this: it wasn't your fault. You were doing the best you could and we're all wired to unconsciously choose safety above all else. It's how we survive.

But also know this: just because you weren't able to take the leap yesterday doesn't mean that you'll go without today. There are opportunities coming your way all the time and, if you miss one, another will come in its place. The trick is to be open to seeing them and being courageous enough to follow them.

I truly believe that the universe is self-organising and self-correcting. I don't know what would have happened if I'd followed my soul's knowing and moved to Bolivia. What I do know is that when the opportunity to move to Portugal presented itself to me a few years later, I found the bravery to follow it. And from that decision, everything started to slot into place for me, perhaps as was intended. The universe didn't punish me for not having previously followed the signs she was giving me. Instead, she gently kept nudging me until, eventually, I listened and took action.

There's no doubt about it, it takes courage and commitment to live a meaningful life. I know from experience that bravery usually comes when our current is experience is so painful and harmful that we have no choice but to leave it. But we don't always have to wait for that. We can choose our own liberation before things get bad. Either way, by committing to our own freedom, our destination — emancipation — is inevitable.

ILLUMINATE & TRANSCEND
End of Chapter Contemplations

Contemplation is the process of bringing something into our awareness and allowing the light of our consciousness to reveal the layers of its meaning to us time and time again. It encourages true transformation by providing space for us to gain deeper clarity on our insights and integrate them into our lives.

You can contemplate through journalling or by going for a walk in nature and asking yourself the question over and over again.

Don't rush through this process. Give yourself space and time for the wisdom to emerge and you'll be blown away by what you discover.

Here are the contemplative prompts for this chapter:

- What resonated with you throughout these pages?

- What have been your biggest breakthrough realisations so far?

- How can you begin to embody the priestess?

EMANCIPATION

There's no mission or goal that is too big. When a woman is dialled into her purpose and opens herself to receive, anything becomes possible in her life. And not only that, she becomes an agent for huge social and planetary change.

Emancipation is the process of liberating ourselves from a system that does not love us. We free ourselves by choosing to take an active role in putting our gifts out into the world and allowing ourselves to receive in return. This is the process of allowing ourselves to thrive — emotionally, spiritually and financially — and using our power to create heaven here on earth. Priestesshood needs a tangible outlet — we must always follow our callings. I personally chose entrepreneurship. Channelling my priestesshood and working for myself has been a powerful access point for truly experiencing healing, freedom, wealth, purpose and impact. In this part of the book, I share with you how I found the courage to follow my callings, finally making the power of the priestess flesh. In the process, I healed and transcended the fear of being truly myself.

LEAVING THE RAT RACE

Once I had left academia, I took a job for a travel operator specialising in archaeological tours. On paper, the job was a dream — creating exciting itineraries in places like South America and South Africa and getting opportunities to lead groups on tour. In reality, it meant being sat in a stuffy office in front of a computer for nine hours a day and occasionally leaving the office to manage tour groups.

If that wasn't suffocating enough, I found myself getting increasingly pissed off with head office who took a top-down managerial approach. This meant that as staff, we were micro-managed at every opportunity, and any creative impulse or innovative spark that we had was immediately stamped out.

I couldn't breathe. The sense of dread upon waking up in the morning, the long commutes, and the feeling that I was wasting my life, became too much. A year later, I quit. I had hardly any savings and no idea what I was going to do next, but I knew that if I didn't give myself permission to explore what was calling me, very soon I'd lose sense of my true authentic self.

I was terrified — I'd never been without a plan. But a few months later I'd bought a one-way ticket to the Philippines to teach yoga at a popular resort. When I first arrived, I was riddled with anxiety. I'd only graduated my yoga teacher training a year before and my teaching experience was sporadic at best. I was convinced that I was going to be found out as a fraud.

The evening before my first morning class, I didn't sleep a wink. I turned up to teach incredibly tired, convinced that no-one would show up and I'd look a fool. To my relief, two bright-eyed Filipino women walked up to the yoga deck. I started with a guided meditation, my voice shaking as a stumbled over my words.

It wasn't the most eloquent class I've ever taught, but I'll never forget the energy of happiness and peace I felt after the class was over. I remember smiling as I contemplated that I had once expected to be a professor, teaching hundreds of archaeology students in a lecture hall and earning good money. I was now in the Philippines, teaching yoga to two students and I'd just earned less than £5. But in that moment I realised that I had never felt so aligned. I was buzzing. I knew I was exactly where I was supposed to be. For the first time in my life, I was following a calling.

Day by day, my confidence grew. Within just a few months, my classes were full and I was matching my previous salary by teaching just three hours a day. I couldn't believe it. The rest of the time, I was drinking coconuts on the beach and enjoying the freedom of island life. I felt free.

My yoga classes were pure transformative alchemy and it was something that came effortlessly to me. I was channelling deep timeless wisdom without even realising it. The priestess was making herself known to me and it was pure magic.

It also boggled my mind that I had matched my old salary so easily. Could it really be this easy? This experience flipped an entrepreneurial switch in my brain and I began to experience increasing freedom by sharing my gifts. Before long, I was flexing my entrepreneurial muscles even more and exploring creative parts of myself that I hadn't accessed since I was a child. I began channelling my knowledge of gemstones into making and selling yoga jewellery. I began to learn that it's a lot easier to make money than I had previously believed, and it could also be a lot more fun.

Having spent my whole life surrounded by academics or people working in traditional 9-5 jobs, I had no idea that there was another way to live. Which is why one of the most pivotal moments in my life was meeting Kayla. A yogi from California, she moved to the Philippines a couple of months after I did and we immediately hit it off. Athletic and petite with beautiful big brown eyes and an infectious smile, I loved her from the outset. Every time we hung out, I felt sparkly and inspired. I was also initially slightly intimidated by her at first because, at that moment in time, I still put people on pedestals. I did wonder why she wanted to hang around with someone like me, but I pushed past the illusion of not feeling good enough and we became good friends. Not only did my yoga teaching improve immeasurably because of her, but my view of what was possible expanded.

She was the first entrepreneurial-minded friend I had ever had. The founder of a non-profit and a yoga retreat company, she had built a life that revolved around following her callings. Our discussions about what we wanted to create and experience in the world lit a fire under me. Through her, I saw that there was another way to live and vowed there and then never to stuff myself back into a 9-5 box ever again. This is why it's so important to surround ourselves with Expanders, people who dream and do and create what they desire in the world. When we are in the energy of these kinds of people, we can't help but calibrate to them.

PRIESTESS POWER

Call in Your Expanders Sadhana

The people you surround yourself with are incredibly important. The more they inspire you, the more you will grow. This isn't to say that you have to ditch your friends and family and move to LA. But by deliberately surrounding yourself with people who already follow their callings, you'll find it much easier to follow your own.

Use these contemplative prompts to explore:

Who in your life is already an Expander for you? Why?

How can you meet more people that inspire you? What events could you go to? Or how could you meet them online?

Is there anyone online that you look up to? How can you enter into their world even deeper? Do they offer programmes or retreats?

How can you also be your own Expander?

BREAKING FREE FROM THE CAGE

Since my days of academia and 9-5 boredom, I've come to understand why it is that so many of us find the toll of modern-day jobs intolerable. And it boils down to one factor: systems. I didn't realise as I was struggling in academia, and barely keeping my head above the water in a 9-5 job, that there was nothing wrong with me — I just kept finding myself in systems that were not designed to help me thrive as a woman.

For me, the rigid system of academia and the demanding system of corporate didn't allow me to own the fullness of my femininity and creativity. And many women find themselves in the same situation, resistant to staying in such soul-drying systems but terrified to leave.

I believe in radical truth-telling, so I'm going to tell it like it is. If you're reading this and you're thinking 'oh my goodness, that's me', you basically have two choices. You can shake up and break up the system that you're in by being yourself unapologetically, demanding change and asking for what you desire so that you can follow your callings and thrive. Or you can leave and create your own path. I personally chose the latter, and stepping into entrepreneurship has been such a gift to me. I have learned that once we give ourselves permission to rewrite the limiting beliefs we have about our capabilities and our worth, there's literally nothing that we cannot create and receive.

I don't believe modern entrepreneurship is for everyone — a woman has to have a certain amount of drive, and if that's not there, it's very difficult to thrive. But I do believe that everyone has entrepreneurial DNA. Before the Industrial Revolution — after which 9-5 life became normalised — many people were farmers, craftspeople or merchants. They didn't rely on a big company for their salary. Instead, they used their skills to contribute to society and make a living. I don't want to over-romanticise this — people's lives before the modern era were far from easy. But people have been using their skills and gifts to make a living for thousands of years. And in today's modern world, where we have tools and knowledge available at our fingertips, it's far easier than it ever was to do this, if we're brave enough to own our fate, follow our callings and own our priestesshood.

There's no mission or goal that is too big. When a woman is dialled into her purpose and opens herself to receive, anything becomes possible in her life. And not only that, she becomes an agent for huge social and environmental change.

JUST DO THE DAMN THING

The truth is that it was only when I decided to come out of the closet and follow my calling to become a women's mentor that I really began honouring and embodying the priestess. To do this I had to own fully and share with the world, who I am and what I'm here to do. In the process of putting myself out there, I've learned how to share my voice (even when I'm shaking), I've become clearer on my dharma, more confident in my skills, my sense of value has increased and my capacity for abundance has become magnified. None of this would have been possible if I hadn't followed my calling and made it my mission to live my purpose.

Building my business has been a powerful vehicle for self-actualisation. I fully owned my priestesshood the moment I decided I was done with my own incessant bullshit. It was the moment I owned my desires and acknowledged that I wanted to be a women's mentor, that I wanted to work less than 20 hours a week, that I wanted to spend my time writing and creating, and that I wanted to get paid well for it, to give back to those less privileged than me, and make more conscious consumer choices. For so long I had waited to feel confident. But confidence is a result of taking massive scary leaps. In response to this recognition, I took the leap by holding free intuitive guidance sessions for women. This scared the pants off me but I had many yoga students who were in need of guidance. I decided to do it for them.

I learned that my experience in the New Age shop, as a yoga teacher, as a PhD researcher, as a tour guide, and as a woman, had already prepared me. And, as I sat down to guide my first session, although I was shaky and a little unsure, I discovered — surprise, surprise — that mentoring came naturally to me. I was able to let my intuition guide me in the direction we needed to go. I learned that the answers are always within the hearts of my clients and my job was simply to point them back to this wisdom. I was born to do this work — as I held more sessions and gained more experience, it felt that facilitating this magic was effortless and I'd finish sessions feeling unbelievably lit.

It would have been easy to turn this calling into a hobby. But I knew if I did that, I'd be playing small. I decided to commit myself and so invested all of my savings into an online business programme. It was scary, but there was something about that decision to commit financially that opened up a portal for it and it spurred me on. Within three months I'd made back that investment, and within the space of six months, I was generating consistent clients. I was in my element and although there were days when I doubted myself and wanted to quit (in fact, that still happens from time to time!), more often than not it felt like the sky was the limit!

MAKING FRIENDS WITH UNCERTAINTY

I've realised that the majority of women who desire to quit their jobs to follow their callings but don't are desperately trying to avoid uncertainty. Certainty is a fundamental human need and we will do everything we can to create it. Patriarchal society conditions people to believe that certainty and security can only be provided by the system. This is why people are scared to leave their jobs — they have more trust in the companies that they work for than they do in their own resourcefulness. This disempowering narrative is the reason why people stay small and stuck. It's why women never fully own their priestesshood and create freedom-based lives. They perceive leaving as too uncertain and so they never take the risk.

The real truth is that nothing external to us is certain. The job, the house, the marriage, the savings — it can all be taken away from you in an instant. These things may make you feel secure and safe but they are illusions. I have learned that the real source of certainty can only ever be found within. We must connect to our personal power and recognise that the source of our power is only ever us. Without risk, there is no magic. We must be willing to leave our comfort zones time and time again.

I now believe with every fibre of my being that whatever comes my way, not only am I able to handle it, but I'm resourceful enough to alchemise it into treasure. The death of my brother taught me that even death can be a gift. That's not to say that I'm unafraid of loss and failure. I'm human and I still fear it. But I know that if and when it comes, to the best of my ability, I will strive to turn it into a lesson and a stepping stone to greater expansion. I choose to dance with uncertainty and be the source of my own power because it's the only way to truly live. This is the priestess's way.

PRIESTESS POWER

Understanding Your Unique Priestesshood Sadhana

Owning your priestesshood and emancipating yourself from systems that do not serve you or your dharma requires clarity, courage and devotion.

Contemplate the following questions and allow them to help you to illuminate your own unique priestesshood:

What is it you feel you're here for? What is calling you?

What do you see other people doing that you wish you could do?

What current systems are you operating in that you know aren't serving you? What keeps you there?

What do you need to believe about yourself and what's possible to break free?

What are the next steps, big or small?

IT'S ALREADY WITHIN YOU

Like I said before, one of the biggest lies that holds a woman back from stepping into her divine-given role of priestess, whether that's facilitating healing, guiding, teaching or creating, is the belief that she's not qualified or she doesn't know enough. This is such bullshit. Everything you need to start is already within you. And what you don't know, you'll learn along the way.

To give you an example, intuition has now become my greatest ally, not only in my life decisions but with how I guide my clients. And intuition is an innate power that we cultivate, not something that is external to us.

When I first started facilitating my work, I became obsessed with learning every tool I could. On one hand, I do believe it's extremely important to develop our skills, but the real reason that I kept looking for new approaches and ways of working with my clients was because I didn't fully trust my own perception. Thanks to a culture that gaslights its women, I found myself doubting my instincts. But once I promised myself to honour my intuition, the work I did with my clients became even more expansive and effortless.

Intuition is more potent than any certification. When I'm with one of my women, I'm the embodiment of the priestess. I listen to the subtle signals of my body as she talks. I make note of the images that come into my mind. And then I share everything I feel and see, mirroring it all back to her. More often than not, it's spot on, and as a consequence, we go deeper and speak truer. It's easy. It's effortless. It's magic.

The Power of the Priestess — Client Spotlight

When my client, Lileth, first started working with me, she struggled with imposter syndrome. A bright and bubbly Dutch woman, with thick brown hair and a warm smile, she had left her full-time job to focus on her business. Within just a year she had launched a thriving podcast and was building a loyal community online. Women were loving the work that she was putting out there for free. The issue was, she wanted to go all-in with her business and start making money in exchange for her work. She wanted to offer intuitive guidance but was terrified of not being qualified enough. In fact, when she spoke to her parents about it, they questioned if she was even allowed to charge for mentoring women. This caused her to spiral and doubt herself even more.

During our time together she came to see that her previous teaching and co-ordinating experience in her past jobs made her more than qualified. And when she did eventually summon up the courage to offer her first mentoring session, she sent me a message straight afterwards to let me know how powerful and energising it was. She was buzzing.

Lileth simply had to give herself permission to explore and lean in to her discomfort. Once she'd dipped her toe in the water, she was able to recognise that she had the inner power all along and that the skills and lessons life had afforded her were already more than enough.

REWRITING YOUR RELATIONSHIP TO FAILURE

For most of my life, I've been terrified of failing. It's not unsurprising. Our culture has a bias towards success — it's reported on, celebrated and strived for. In contrast, failure is seen as something shameful. And because we fear judgement, we fear failure.

The fear of failure is a trauma adaption, a response of the nervous system to keep you away from perceived danger. To your primitive brain, failure and death are synonymous. But in the modern world, it's unlikely that you will die if your book gets a bad review or your product or service doesn't initially sell. It might feel embarrassing. It might feed some limiting beliefs that you have about yourself. But it won't kill you.

A powerful way to move past the fear of failure is to celebrate your failures. Why? Because it signals that you've been brave enough to take messy and uncomfortable action in the direction of your desires and dharma. Most people never do this. Most people talk about all the things that they'd like to do one day. But they never do it.

What we need to understand and embody is that failure isn't the opposite of success. It's a stepping stone to it. Without failure, we don't learn. Without failure, we don't grow. Without failure, we cannot succeed. I've learned that we can only truly fail if we stop trying. By committing ourselves to keep going until we break through, our failure is simply feedback and an opportunity to discover what works for us.

Let me give you a very tangible example. Despite having had success in filling up my one-to-one client spaces early on in my business, when I first launched a group programme, it completely flopped. One person applied and I actually had to cancel the programme. I felt like a failure. But I decided I was going to keep going no matter what. Less than a few months later, armed with what I'd learned, I launched and filled another programme. And now when I launch programmes, not only do they always fill, but they change women's lives, which is the whole point. We have to believe that our success is inevitable. We don't get to be in charge of how long it takes — that's not for us to decide. But as long as we keep going and we don't give up, success will come.

The question is: how much do you really want this? How much do you want to live a life that's true to you? How much do you want to honour your creativity and your callings? How much do you desire to liberate yourself and others? You have to be tenacious. You have to be obsessed. You have to understand that it takes as long as it takes and often you'll be failing before you're succeeding. Sometimes, success comes effortlessly. Other times, it doesn't. However it pans out, failure is your friend. Remember that Thomas Edison 'failed' hundreds of times before successfully inventing the lightbulb and now, because he didn't give up, the whole world is illuminated. Imagine what would be possible if you fully committed to showing up for your desires and dharma, no matter what. Imagine how different your life would be.

The Power of the Priestess — Client Spotlight

Emma, a fiery redhead from the UK, desperately wanted to create a successful coaching business. When I asked her why she wanted this in one of our mentoring sessions, she admitted that she still felt that she had something to prove. It was tearing her up inside because rather than truly enjoying the process of building her business, she was constantly fretting about what she would do if it didn't work. What would people think of her? How would she explain it?

As I write this, this realisation for Emma is still fresh, and perhaps as it has been for me, it will be a lengthy process of de-conditioning herself from the need for external approval. Yet illumination is often our biggest victory in the battle against our internalised cages of oppression, because when we can see our patterns clearly, we can become more aware of how they rob us of joy and the soulful fulfilment we seek. I have no doubt that, as she commits to her journey, she will learn to unhook herself from the need for external validation and instead create a life and business that satisfies her soul.

THERE ARE NO GURUS

I'm 26 years old and sat listening to my spiritual teacher, Satyananda. There are about twenty-five of us sat together in satsang, which is Sanskrit for a group of people gathered to speak spiritual truth. Satyananda is leading the conversation and as he is speaking, I can't quite shake off the feeling that it's time for me to leave the community.

I'd been studying with Satyananda for four years. When I first found him, I was vulnerable and impressionable. I saw him as an enlightened being and I lapped up all his teachings without question. But as time went on, I started questioning the way the community was run. The issue for me was that within the community, there wasn't much space to question him and his teachings. This is the biggest issue I see with a lot of spiritual teachers. Gaslighting, in the form of spiritual bypassing and labelling someone's legitimate concerns as the product of their ego, is a convenient and effective way of exerting control over members of a spiritual community.

I'm not saying that what was happening in our community was sinister. I know in my heart that Satyananda deeply believed in what he was teaching and that he genuinely wanted freedom for all. But I still felt uncomfortable because a space where people cannot hold their leaders accountable or call their leaders out is fertile ground for abuse of power. And far from empowering people, is disempowers them to look for the answers externally, rather than searching for the wisdom within. I believe the only real guru is the guru within — the inner felt sense of wisdom and intuition. And rather than give us all the answers, the true role of a teacher is to point us back to seek the answers within.

A NEW PARADIGM OF LEADERSHIP

One of my favourite personal mantras is: 'I'm a woman in process'. It reminds me that the idea that I have to have it all figured out is an illusion. It also gives me permission to let go of right or wrong, good or bad, and simply explore.

The priestess demands us to step into our leadership. Notice how your body responds when you read this. Do you feel expansive or is there the constriction of fear telling you that leadership isn't for you? A few years ago, I would never have believed that I had what it took to be a leader. There were two reasons for this.

First, I hadn't learned how to lead myself. I was very good at sharing excellent advice. But I wasn't so good at following it myself, which meant that I was completely out of integrity with the woman I wanted to be. When it comes to leadership, integrity is everything, and to be congruent, we have to do as we say. We must embody our leadership and lead by example. Now, as best I can, I don't share any approaches or practices with my clients that I haven't integrated myself. I deeply embody what I teach whilst paradoxically realising that I have a lot to learn and unlearn. More on this later.

The second was that I associated leadership with white middle-class men who were led by their egos. Or spiritual leaders who were full of ego. I saw them as corrupted by power and unwilling to bring about real justice and social change.

When the priestess first nudged me towards leadership, I had a lot to unlearn. I initially subscribed to a very traditional model of leadership and was convinced that it was about knowing more than others and telling people what to do and how to do it. Stepping into my priestesshood meant I had to embrace leadership and at first this was deeply uncomfortable. Like so many of us, initially, I wore the mask of perfectionism, believing that this was the only way to show up in my power. But I soon felt tired of this facade. I longed to be myself and not feel I had to hide the human parts of myself that I'd been taught were messy and unloveable.

I was also tired of seeing others showing up in their leadership as if they had all the answers. Rather than empowering me, I would watch them and feel completely inadequate. Seeing them in their perfection led me to wonder if I was the only one who was experiencing 'bad' days. Seeing them in their glossy perfection instilled within me with the dangerous belief that one day, if I worked hard enough, I would be perfect and have it all figured out, and that until then, I was below standard and lacking.

Thankfully it didn't take me long to realise that everything I was seeing was complete bullshit. These people didn't have it all figured out. Instead, they had chosen to project a carefully constructed image of themselves. This is what we've all been taught to do. When we fear that we are not enough, we become actresses, playing the role that we think people want us to play. It's only when we take the final bow that we realise the audience is clapping for a make-believe character and not who we really are deep down. This is not success nor is it liberation.

Despite popular opinion, I decided it would be much more expansive for me, and for my women, to show up as myself. As soon as I did, I felt much more in integrity. Yet, even these days, as I show up and candidly share my struggles and messiness, women often message me to share with me how brave they think I am. Somewhere in the subtext of these messages, there's always the implication that I courageously share my vulnerabilities at the expense of my image and leadership. Somehow, collectively, we still believe that being honest and open is weakness. Yet, since I made the conscious choice to show up more authentically with my community, not only have I felt freer but I have noticed it acts as a catalyst for the liberation of others. It turns out that women desire to align themselves with leaders that they can relate to, human to human. I've learned that strong leadership is actually about vulnerability — there's no courage, growth or trust without it. And to lead powerfully, we must first trust that we are enough just as we are.

Our world doesn't need more polished people pretending to have their shit together. We need more people to own their experience of life, drop into their hearts, and have the capacity to have uncomfortable conversations. True leadership is to help people see that there's nothing wrong with them and that all the answers they ever need are within. Always. I now make it my mission to show the women who enter into my spaces that I'm just like them and they're just like me — women in process. There's no destination that we have to get to. Often the only difference between them and me is that I keep choosing my priestesshood even when the inner voices are screaming at me all the reasons that I shouldn't.

Non-hierarchical leadership is the kind of leadership that holds space for people to share and create their own solutions. We can't facilitate the empowerment of others if we're preaching to them. We can't help people empower themselves if we're on a pedestal looking down. We can only help people rise if we stand with them at the same level and offer them a leg up. To me, this is true leadership and this is what the priestess does. She trusts her people. She trusts Life will take care of it and her only job is to act and be a guardian of Life. She's not grandiose. She's not trying to prove anything. She's not above anyone. She recognises that through compassion, understanding and vulnerability, she catalyses the alchemy of change.

PRIESTESS POWER

Stepping into Your Leadership Sadhana

Living our lives as priestesses is all about summoning up the courage to step into feminine leadership.

Use these contemplation prompts to uncover and explore the ways in which you can boldly claim your leadership:

What does real leadership mean to you?

What are the ways in which you shy away from leadership, and why?

How does you stepping into your feminine leadership benefit yourself and the planet?

What small steps can you take to lead yourself and become a powerful leader to others?

USING YOUR PRIVILEGE

When it comes to unleashing our feminine power and creating an amazing life, we're not all starting from the same place. Yes, we all have the power to create our destiny, yet some of us are born with more advantages than others. Privilege is a fact of life. We all have it. And yet somehow we've been conditioned to turn a blind eye to it and instead play the victim. When we play the victim, no matter how subtle it is, we're not taking responsibility for our experience of life. Period. The priestess acknowledges her privilege and uses it to be an advocate for social justice and healing.

First and foremost, some of you reading this have white or light-coloured skin, just like me. White supremacy, just like patriarchy, is a system of oppression that is alive and kicking. Even though I didn't ask for it, I have benefitted from it. Some of you have other notable privileges such as being cisgender, meaning that your sense of gender identity corresponds with your sex. You may be well-educated. You may be thin. You may be beautiful. Aspects such as these have afforded you huge privilege in your life because these are certain aspects of your identity that match social norms or expectations.

Privilege is multi-layered and multi-faceted. Every single one of us without exception has privilege in some form. And with privilege there is power. I believe it's the duty of every person on this planet, regardless of gender, to use their gifts to benefit humanity as well as to speak out about injustice and call attention to the misuse of power. Women in particular have been taught not to use their privilege. We fear judgement. We fear condemnation. We fear belittlement. And so we keep our mouths shut. Never has this been more painfully apparent than in the personal development world. The tendency to focus only on light and love and spread 'good vibes only' is a type of spiritual gaslighting that allows privileged people to stay in their privileged bubble. Evolution from this place is about the goals of the individual rather than the elevation of the collective.

Our privilege is not something we need to feel shame for or beat ourselves up about — we didn't create the system. Instead, it's more powerful to contemplate how we can use the privilege that we have to help others with less.

Women are the greatest untapped resource. Right now there are so many brilliant ideas locked up inside the hearts of women, kept closely guarded under lock and key because of systemic conditioning. That's roughly 50% of the population who have been conditioned to keep their mouths shut. This means that not only are so many women not living the lives they deeply desire to, but also that global social and environmental injustice is not sufficiently addressed because we fear speaking out and being persecuted for it. We have the fire of sacred activism in our hearts, but we live in a system that discourages us from fanning its flames. How convenient.

What would the world look like if more conscientious, compassionate and ethical women freed themselves up to create and express what their heart is yearning for? What if they had received the message that it's okay to shine, it's okay to be bold, it's okay to be powerful and it doesn't make you a bitch or arrogant to lead? What then? How would our society look? How would our planet look? Because, as long as women keep listening to messages that they should not take a seat at the table, our planet will continue to suffer. Children will continue to suffer. Adults will continue to suffer. The environment will continue to suffer.

We must use whatever privilege we have. It's time to love ourselves and our planet so fiercely that we do whatever it takes to free ourselves from the discrimination and self-hatred. Now is our time. More than ever. We are needed — every single one of us.

SACRED ACTIVISM

As I stepped into my priestesshood and built my mentoring business, I realised very quickly that my goal wasn't only to serve women of affluent means, no matter how important that work is. I wanted my dharma to have a wider impact. This meant learning how to ensure that my business didn't perpetuate the systemic and environmental issues I want humanity to transcend and this has meant taking a long hard look in the mirror.

The biggest thing that pisses me off about the spiritual community is that many turn a blind eye to social and environmental injustice. They may share the odd post on social media, but then they get back to burning their sage and drinking matcha lattes, falsely believing that there's nothing they can do about the state of the world. There is a dangerous lie within spiritual circles that if we speak about something, we give energy to it. This is wrong. We have to be brave enough to illuminate shadow because it's only when we see something clearly that we can transcend it. And often, it's going to look really ugly.

The rhetoric of 'good vibes only' and the advice to 'focus only on the light' is incredibly harmful. Internally, it means we reject our shadowy emotions and, in doing so, we actually give them more power. Externally, it means that there are groups of people living at the social margins, and declining ecosystems, needing our help, who we refuse to acknowledge.

I believe as priestesses it's our duty to get political and share our voice. In my opinion, there are too many spiritual teachers out there who bypass politics because it's 'low vibe' or 3D. What a load of shit. This speaks more about their privilege than anything else. In priestesshood, there has to be space for duality. We must focus on the elevation of consciousness and address social and environmental injustice because none of us are fully free until the whole planet is free.

Sacred activism is about speaking out. It's about being willing to challenge the attitudes of the status quo. It's about being willing to get it wrong. It's about letting go of the need to be liked and choosing to say what needs to be said. It's about putting the rights of marginalised people above our own feelings of guilt and shame. It's about learning about how our unconscious behaviours are contributing to the destruction of entire ecosystems. It's about signing petitions. It's about offering our listening ear to learn. It's about offering our time and resources. It's about consciously choosing how we spend money (more on this later). It's about following our hearts and doing what's just, not what's easy. In essence, it's about using any privilege that we have to make a difference. We must remember that we are the system and that what we do matters. Systems only maintain their power if people keep acting in the same ways that they have always acted. For change to occur, we must act in integrity with our inner values.

PRIESTESS POWER

Uncovering Your Core Values Sadhana

We all have underlying core values and when they become conscious, we can use them to navigate the decisions that we make in our lives.

A core value is simply something that is important to you.

Examples of my core values are authenticity, truth, freedom, rebellion, revolution, and peace.

Use these contemplation prompts to uncover and explore your core values:

Think of a meaningful and happy memory in your past. What was happening and how did you feel? What values were you honouring?

Now think of an upsetting memory in your past. What was happening and how did you feel? What values were not being honoured?

What's important for you in your life?

What do you believe in? Equal rights for all? Sustainability? Peace? Where in your life are you not living in alignment with what you say you believe in and how can you rectify this?

BEFRIENDING MONEY

I'm 13 years old and I've just had a huge argument with my dad. He's just told me that he can't afford to send me on the annual school trip. At first, I believed him, but then I overheard a conversation between him and my mum where I learned that they do have the money, he just didn't think it was worth it.

I'm lying on my bed, burying my head into my pillow and sobbing big fat salty tears. I'm torn because I love my dad and I don't want to be a burden to him. On the other hand, I just want to feel like a normal kid for a change. I know that the next few weeks are going to feel like agony as my school friends excitedly chat about their upcoming trip. All I want is to feel that I'm worthy of having the same experiences as my friends. But I don't. I feel like a sad, pathetic, poor loser.

These are the sorts of experiences that shape our relationship with money. My mum and dad had very different attitudes to money. My mum was never able to save much but she believed in spending money on herself and others. My dad was the opposite. He believed that money was hard to come by and that there was never enough, and he experienced redundancies and challenges as a freelancer that solidified these beliefs. He worked hard for his money and his fear of one day running out and not being able to support his family meant that he was extremely frugal, even in times when there was no need to be. As a child, of course, I didn't understand this. I simply believed that people like us don't have a lot of money and that money was hard to come by. As a result, I spent 30 years of my life basing most of my decisions on perceived scarcity rather than perceived abundance.

This all changed in my early 30s. Channelling my priestesshood into building a business has been one of the most liberating and challenging experiences of my life. I went from living a life where someone else decided how much money I could earn in a year, to being in total control of my work and financial destiny. I've also learned that a woman can't be truly empowered without looking at and up-levelling her relationship with money. And working for yourself is an incredible vehicle to do just that. The only limits to the money you can generate as an entrepreneur are the limits that you choose, and this means taking radical responsibility for your financial situation.

Money talk triggers the hell out of people. If I write a social media post about money or send out an email about it, my unfollow and unsubscribe rates spike without fail. I believe this is because, for most of us, we see money as something that's dirty or evil, and we judge others who have it or desire it. We believe that wanting money is wrong. And yet we also wish that we had more of it because we desire to feel secure and abundant. As a result, most of us find ourselves in conflict, barely getting by, making poor decisions for the well-being of the planet, or making choices for our lives that ignore our soul callings in favour of the perceived safety of a steady pay cheque.

Money itself isn't dirty or bad. Money is inherently neutral. When looked at logically, it's obvious that money is simply a value of exchange. It's a number. Curiously, there aren't enough coins and notes in circulation to account for all the money that 'exists' in the world. Money is simply a number in a bank account and isn't physical. When I finally understood this, it blew my mind. Money therefore is simply a system that we buy into. It holds power because we believe it does.

What if I were to ask you 'what does money represent to you?' Most likely you would say something along the lines of 'freedom'. We think this. We think that money represents freedom. But in our current capitalist set-up, for most of us, it actually represents scarcity. Many of us are using the excuse of money not to do the things that light us up. We tell ourselves that we need to stay in our soul-sucking jobs rather than following our callings because of money. Or more accurately, an idea of how available we think money is. And there are some of us that overspend on resources that we don't need and end up racking up debt. This is not freedom either.

The Power of the Priestess - Client Spotlight

Becca had grown up believing that in order to create security for herself, she needed a stable job and six-figure income. This meant that she had spent almost a decade of her life working in a bank. It was a respectable job but something was missing. She became drawn to yoga and quickly got her teaching certification.

When we started working together, she was still working at the bank, but it was draining her and leaving her very little time to follow her calling to share her love for yoga and personal development. Yet, within a couple of weeks of actively working with the energy of the priestess, Becca decided to quit her job. Although she was terrified, she knew deep down that the security her job gave her was an illusion. The reality was that the job wasn't giving her safety, it was keeping her caged.

The same week that she quit her job, she landed herself a full schedule of yoga teaching at a local studio. And within a few months, she was filling up her yoga courses and women's circles. It wasn't yet the six-figure salary she was used to, but it was more than enough.

Becca learned that she had previously been using money as an excuse not to follow her dharma. As she connected to her inner priestess, found her courage and took big leaps, opportunities and resources came to her exactly as they were needed. And the universe continued to reward her faith and devotion to her inner guidance.

MONEY MIRRORS YOUR RELATIONSHIP WITH LIFE

Each of us has an internal wealth baseline. This is the amount of wealth that feels familiar and comfortable to us. We sometimes dip below the baseline. Sometimes we experience moments when we're above our baseline. But very quickly we return to what feels familiar and safe. This is why lottery winners often declare themselves bankrupt within a few years. But we can easily change our relationship to money, we just have to decide to.

I want to share with you an example of how shifting our relationship with money shifts our relationship to life. A few months into starting my mentoring business my parents came to Portugal to visit me and Mauro. I paid for their dinners without worrying — this was something I'd never done before without feeling anxiety. And I wasn't necessarily doing it because I had more money in the bank. It was because I had started to understand that as long as I kept taking scary action towards my callings and dharma, the universe would always provide for me.

Embodying the priestess has truly helped me allow myself to ask and receive. The priestess is a vessel of the Divine and a channel through which healing and transcendence flows. And money is energy. Therefore the role of the priestess is to treat herself as a servant of the Divine and direct energy (money) where it needs to flow.

When it comes to money, I've learned that it's powerful to get practical and there are certain principles and rituals that we can live by to encourage more financial abundance to flow. First, feeling gratitude for what we have and what's to come is powerful. Saying thank you when we receive, no matter how small, shifts a lot. We can say thank you when we pay someone or buy something, feeling into the beautiful fact that we have the resources to access food. We can imagine where that money is going to go, who it's going to help. We can know that it will come back to us. We can give thanks for compliments and free drinks. We can appreciate everything anyone does for us and notice that opportunities and resources keep coming our way. Initially, we have to train ourselves to do this but after a while it becomes habit. I'm now forever spontaneously saying thank you to everything that flows to me and everything that I'm able to give back.

Second, the law of circulation states that we receive what we give out. We can start by buying our friends coffee or giving to charities that resonate with our values. I make a point to regularly donate to causes that align with the values of my business, particularly causes that help people living in the margins of society and the environment. We have to remember that money flows through us and the way to receive it is to get it flowing. This needs to happen from a sense of overflow, not obligation. It doesn't always matter how much we give, it's the act of giving that counts. Whatever we give out will come back to us in kind. If we want someone to support our small business, we must support someone else's small business. If we want our boss to appreciate us, we must appreciate our boss (no matter how challenging). This is embodying wealth.

Third is to focus on our resourcefulness. The source of our ability to create money is within us. Money itself can be taken away from us in a moment. But no-one can take away our talent, drive, knowledge, creativity and mission. Our external abundance will always match how much we're tapped into our inner sense of wealth. We need to train ourselves to look for evidence that we are resourceful and can not only handle anything that comes our way but make it a triumph. We must constantly look for evidence that our success is inevitable.

Fourth, cultivating our sense of worth as women raises our

wealth consciousness. When we feel valuable, we show up differently in the world. We are able to ask for what we want and we increase our capacity to receive. It starts with the small things, like when someone offers to do something for us. Rather than deflect their help, which so many of us do, we can graciously receive it and train ourselves to receive everything that comes our way, knowing that we are worthy of it.

And finally, by doing things that excite us and scare us, we pave the way for opportunities and resources to come. We must take action on the things that light us up, especially if they don't make logical sense. These are signposts from the universe to lean in. When we let go of obligation and jump into doing things that feel exhilarating and take us out of our comfort zone, magic happens. Prosperity is always on the other side of this when we open ourselves up to receive it.

When it comes to money, our biggest danger lies in the over-identification with it. We've been taught that our value is related to our income, assets and achievements, which means we feel good when we have it but bad when we don't. And, in attempts to keep our money and status, this can lead us to make a lot of decisions that are out of integrity with what we truly desire. We must remember that money is simply a tool and not the source of our worth. It's not even the source of our wealth — the source of our wealth is our inner magic and natural world. Money is a tool that we can direct so that we live the lives we wish to and contribute to the lives of others. It's only when we are mastering money, rather than being mastered by it, that we can truly say it gives us freedom.

YOU'RE ALLOWED TO RECEIVE

Money is energy. It represents value, attention and power. There's a reason why Donald Trump sits in the Oval Office as I write this. He understands money and he used it to buy and manipulate his way into the White House. Money is neutral, but when it's in the hands of people with black hearts, corruption follows. We somehow believe that money is the problem, but money reflects and amplifies what's already within a human. If you're a good person, having access to more money will not change that. In fact, it will amplify the good that you can do in the world.

The biggest lie we tell ourselves about money is that the 1% (the richest people in the world) are more powerful than the 99%. We believe that they are the ones who hold all the power. And because we believe this, we go about our days like sheep, believing that our individual choices don't matter. This is why the majority of the middle classes still opt-in to buy cheap factory clothes from China, cheap meat from supermarkets, and cheap plastic objects that can't be recycled. And why do they continue to make these choices, choosing cheap over ethical, regardless of what's in their bank accounts? Because they believe in scarcity more than their responsibility. This goes for the majority of us who believe that there isn't enough money and we have to conserve and save. Now, of course, this doesn't apply to everyone. There are people living in poverty and of course they're going to do everything they can to keep costs down and provide for themselves and their family. In their state of survival, the environment seems less of a concern. This is not their fault. It's the fault of the system.

It's not the 1% that's destroying our planet. It's the consumer. If there was no consumer demand, businesses would go out of business within a fortnight. We owe it not only to ourselves but to our planet to bring ourselves out of poverty consciousness. This is a mindset shift. Most of us think, 'I'll buy more ethical products or I'll give to charity when I have the money.' This thinking is part of the problem. We wait for our physical circumstances to change, not realising that our internal world must change first. We mistakenly believe that having more money will make us feel wealthy, but that's backward thinking. Money doesn't create feelings of wealth. Feelings of wealth create abundance.

In the past few years, I've learned how to create financial wealth as a priestess. And as a result, my choices continue to be in integrity with my values. Not 100% of the time of course — I'm still learning — but more and more. I decided to start making these choices before my financial situation changed. These decisions included: buying lunch for friends who were earning less, making sure we bought local produce regardless of the price, choosing to offset our carbon footprint every time we flew somewhere, donating to causes we believed in, and choosing to contribute to other local businesses. These actions were rooted in abundance, not scarcity, and soon enough money started flowing more and I was able to give back more and more. This is prosperity consciousness — realising that our wealth and what we do with it has a huge impact on the state of the planet and that the more we give the more we receive.

We can use our wealth to help others and the environment. Yet I'm also a big believer in a woman choosing to experience sustainable comfort and luxury — we don't need to selflessly sacrifice and give everything away. My needs and the needs of my family are still my biggest priority because when I'm looked after, I'm far more useful to the planet. I've had to do a lot of inner work to feel that way. A woman's ability to ask for and receive is always underpinned by her sense of value and worth. And for a long time, I did not believe that I was valuable.

My hope is that, as you read this, you begin to recognise the important role that you play in the healing of our planet. And I hope that you begin to understand that by committing to not letting money be the excuse for why you don't follow your callings, and committing to receiving more wealth in your life and living your values with that wealth, you can make a huge difference.

CAPITALISM NEEDS A MAKEOVER

When I was 16 years old I fell in love with punk music. There was something about the rebellion against the establishment and the call for anarchy that resonated with me deeply. Wearing Doc Martens, listening to The Clash, reading Karl Marx, and kissing all the alternative boys were my ways of aligning myself with an ideology that represented what I felt to be true. At 16, I wasn't able to eloquently articulate why I was so against the system. But I knew at a fundamental level that the way society was put together was oppressive. Since then, I've been able to channel this teenage angst into a more concrete understanding: capitalism as it exists today is destroying our planet and society. If we want our planet to survive and our people to thrive, capitalism needs a makeover.

The issue with the capitalist system is that it's solely driven by financial profit. This blinkered focus has created global chaos such as the destruction of the entire ecosystems, social inequality, and corruption of power. I'm not against capitalism. But I believe that it's time to reinvent it. For that, we need to understand both its shortcomings and how we as priestesses can be part of the solution.

How would our world look and operate if we focused not just on financial profit but other forms of growth measurement? It's my belief and experience that there are multiple currencies besides money. Money is not something to reject, but it's only one currency of abundance and growth. Other currencies of true prosperity include energy, water, nutritious food, time, well-being, fulfilment, connection and love.

Our society has a very limited view of what success is. True success is mostly synonymous with achievement, status and financial gain. I believe that the concept of the American Dream is ingrained within almost everyone living with Western culture, whether they are in the US or not. Central to this concept is the idea that if you work hard enough and follow a set path, you will become materially 'successful'. The belief here is that the more you have materially, the happier you will feel. It's the main driving force of our current economy — make people feel like they are lacking and encourage them to strive for big houses, big cars, and designer clothes.

There's nothing wrong with having access to wealth and enjoying sustainable luxury — I'm all for it. But if it's at the expense of other currencies of true abundance, we will find ourselves out of balance, in the toxic sea of over-achievement and external validation. When we believe our worth is related to what we do, rather than who we are, it creates issues. The number of struggling celebrities, CEOs and high-achievers is on the rise. Under more pressure than 'ordinary people', many suffer from panic attacks, insomnia, violent outbursts, substance abuse, eating disorders, suicidal thoughts, and addictions. Often they have sacrificed family, romantic relationships and even their health to rise to the top. As a result, their support network tends to be weaker than that of ordinary people.

Often the tendency to over-achieve and accumulate things is a trauma response. In my life, this was evident in my decision to follow the academic path and write a PhD. I knew that it would make my parents proud and I believed that when I was able to call myself doctor, I would finally feel like I was somebody. Of course this didn't happen. On the day I was awarded my doctorate, I cried buckets of tears. The truth was that the piece of paper I was given didn't make me feel like I thought it would. I still didn't feel enough. I still felt inadequate. I still felt like a fraud.

This is the issue with placing so much of our sense of self on external achievement and material assets. When we attain them, they never make us feel whole in the way we think it will.

Western culture teaches us that our external achievements and assets are directly related to our value and worth and many of us feel a need to prove ourselves. Letting ourselves be consumed with the desire for external validation robs us of joy. And it's sneaky. It creeps up on us even when we're trying to avoid it.

In the first few months of my mentoring business, I started seeing huge success and very soon I was fully booked with paying clients who loved the work we were doing together. I was earning more money monthly than I had ever made in my entire life and for a while, I was ecstatic about it. But slowly I noticed how fixated I started to become on my income. I kept sharing with my parents how much I was making, which was bizarre because I was still choosing to live a relatively minimalistic lifestyle, in alignment with my values. Underneath the obsession with the figures was the same pattern that had been there during my PhD years: the desire to be seen as valuable and worthy.

Money needs to be a byproduct of living an aligned and ethical life. What I have found is that when I fully embody my priestesshood, put service at the forefront of everything I do, and chose freedom over expectation, abundance flows to me in all forms, including money. I welcome money into my life more than ever, but not at the expense of my wellbeing. More and more these days, I find myself not having to choose between the two.

What would society look like if we were all willing to measure our success based on how good we felt? Or how much time we had? Or how much energy we had? Or how much love we were experiencing? How would our lives be then?

This is why capitalism needs a makeover, because the pursuit of financial profit and material wealth over everything else is a one-way ticket to individual and collective destruction. The cultivation of all currencies of true prosperity instead allows us to live in harmony with ourselves and each other.

REJECTING GRIND CULTURE

Grind culture is instilled in us from an early age. We believe that the harder we work, the more we will succeed, and the more worthy we will feel. And most of us never even question the assumption that success and hard work go together hand in hand. But is this really true? Do you have to hustle and grind to create your version of success for yourself?

When I was writing my PhD, I shared an office with my postgraduate colleagues. We had an absolutely brilliant time together — there was a lot of laughter during those years. But we also worked extremely hard. Or at least pretended to, when we weren't going down the pub or sneaking out to smoke (I drank a lot and smoked a little back in those days). There was always pressure to work long hours and prove your dedication to your work. I resisted this in the beginning but as time marched on and deadlines loomed, I worked extremely hard. The expectation that a PhD can be written in only three years is ludicrous, and almost no-one manages it. But there I was, grinding to prove myself as an academic and feeling guilty and lazy when I wanted to take the day off. When I worked for the travel operator, it was a similar story. We were paid for eight hours of work a day but most people worked for at least 10 because it was expected of them. Those who chose to only work their set hours were almost never promoted, presumably because their dedication to the company was seen as questionable.

The truth is that we don't have to hustle and grind to experience abundance and success on our terms. Patriarchal society expects women to operate linearly. Linear energy is masculine in nature and our whole society is built on the idea that everyone operates steadily. This creates confusion, disempowerment and frustration because, yes, masculine energy does work like that, but the feminine is receptive and cyclical. There is a natural ebb and flow to everything. When we align with our inner cycles and nature's cycles, rather than ignoring or overriding them, we allow for the forces of nature to facilitate our healing, growth and expansion.

A society that focuses on and is built only upon the masculine is a society that is completely out of balance. This is why so many people burn out. And a larger percentage of these people are women. Why? Because institutions and systems are not built to honour the cyclical feminine and so the feminine cannot thrive. I believe this is why so many women want to leave their jobs.

The hustle and grind culture is a system of oppression and it hits women the hardest. First, globally, three-quarters of all unpaid work is done by women meaning we are expected to do a lot more than our male counterparts. Second, our culture forgets that women are cyclical — our hormones fluctuate throughout the month meaning that our brain chemistry and our energy level are never static. Third, our culture teaches us to override what we feel and what we need. It teaches us that there is no value in rest and that if we're not being productive, we are lazy and worthless. This system, like all systems, becomes internalised, so that even if we do leave our jobs, we still function in accordance with this internal operating system.

Priestess Power — Client Spotlight

Carly is an Italian-American woman with thick brown hair and an infectious laugh. She was simultaneously working corporate world and building her business but was finding it hard to manage her energy. She often felt stressed, anxious and depleted, and realised that this wasn't what she wanted. She wanted freedom and abundance.

As our work together unfolded, she was able to recognise that in her struggle to prove her worth and hustle hard, she had completely neglected her body. As a result, she wasn't enjoying her life. What happened over the next year was incredible. She began to reclaim her body, reclaim her self-care and reclaim herself. She took care of her nutritional health, she gave herself permission to rest and, as a result, not only did she feel amazing, but her business started to thrive. She let her feminine take over from the masculine and, in doing so, freed herself up from the trap of needing to always be productive.

SUCCESS IS THE BYPRODUCT

Following our callings encourages us to confront parts of our conditioning and trauma that are begging to be healed and transcended. Building my mentoring practice has been a huge vehicle for inner healing. Abundance and achievement have simply been the fun byproducts. For me, channelling my priestesshood in this way has helped me heal and grow in so many areas of my life. It's encouraged me to get clear on my mission and dharma. I've healed a lot of my money wounds. I've healed a lot of my trauma related to being judged, rejected or undervalued. I've increased my sense of worth and contribution. My ability to create boundaries has increased dramatically. I've transcended many of my limiting beliefs and stories. And I've learned to embody powerful feminine leadership.

The majority of us have been led to believe that when we feel confident and ready, then we can commit to following what calls us. But this is backward. It's taking the leap that will undoubtedly increase our confidence and create a more empowered sense of self. Confidence comes as a result of consistently being outside of our comfort zone. Over the past few years, I have become more me and experienced more abundance and more fulfilment than ever before. But I have also experienced more discomfort and fear than ever before. If we want to grow in our capacity to experience the expansiveness of living our dharma, we also have to be prepared to face and dance with our shadow. There is no other way.

YOU'RE A MIRROR

Sometimes it's not the fear of failure but the fear of success that holds us back from following our callings. We're not sure if we could handle our success. Or we believe we'd burn out. Or we're not sure if we want the responsibility. Or we worry our friends and family will judge us. Most of us fear that our success will make others feel uncomfortable. We cringe at the idea that our family, friends, or colleagues will watch and judge.

Like I've said before, some people will judge you. But this is not your responsibility or your concern. You're a mirror and any judgements about you are never about you. They are a reflection of the other person, including their beliefs, preferences and wounding. You get to be unapologetically you.

And as a mirror, what if you inspire others? What if you shining gives them permission to also shine, since all you're doing is reflecting back to them their own light? What if they change their whole life because they see you doing it? We cannot say we're here for others and that we want their growth if we're not willing to be the inspiration that catalyses their journey. You playing small doesn't serve anyone. It doesn't serve you and it doesn't serve the people you care about. Embody your message. Show them what's possible. And be a light to the world.

WE GO FURTHER TOGETHER

About three months into my new mentoring business, I had a booked out practice, but I'd also hit a wall with my energy. It was ironic because I was helping my clients reconnect to their feminine magic but, in terms of my business, I was operating almost fully from the masculine.

The biggest lie I was believing was that I was supposed to do it all by myself. I was holding space for a number of women but I was already feeling maxed out in just a few months. I didn't have any more bandwidth for self-care, nor did I have the energy to expand my mission and vision.

In desperation, I reached out to an online community where I was met with the question: 'Sarah, you're supporting a lot of women but who's supporting you?' I was stunned when I realised I wasn't letting myself be supported by anyone. No-one was holding space for me. I felt out of integrity with my message and so, within the space of a week, I'd hired two mentors, one for business and one for my personal life. I also started sharing more with my friends. Suddenly the burden was shared. And my capacity for more increased.

This is how it works. When we allow ourselves to be supported, we automatically embody the receptivity of the feminine. And this is where a lot of the old-school feminist rhetoric gets it all wrong. It's told us that we're independent. It's told us we've got this. It's told us we don't need anyone but ourselves. But far from empowering us, this narrative has done the exact opposite. It has cut us off from the nurturing embrace of the Divine Masculine and the support that is vital for our growth.

The truth is that the concept of independence is an illusion. It takes a village to create anything in this world. Look at the top or shirt you're wearing right now. This item of clothing contains the imprinted traces of many people's input, from the people who designed the style, colour and pattern of the top, to the farmers who grew the cotton, to the factory workers who spun the cotton and sewed the finished article, to the people involved in shipping it to the shop or to your home. Nothing is created or continues to exist in isolation. The process of creation happens through networks of people. Social connections and support are integral to experiencing limitless possibilities and growth. When we don't allow ourselves to ask for and receive support, there is only so far we can stretch.

It wasn't my fault that I'd tried to do everything by myself. Prior to hiring my first mentors, I'd actually had some fairly sad experiences with people in mentoring roles. In particular, I had gone through a traumatic experience with a female member of staff during my university days. This particular staff member did not have my best interests at heart even though she pretended she did. I'll never fully understand why, but I feel that something about me made her feel threatened. Far from playing the part of the wise older sister, she instead assumed the role of the jealous stepmother. She didn't believe I was good enough and she made damn well sure I knew it. Perhaps to her mind her criticisms were a way to toughen me. But they only created pain and suffering, because they triggered my inner wounding. I feel sure that she was unaware of what she was doing and how I was feeling. Or at least I hope so. But this is the danger of putting people into positions of leadership without encouraging them to do deep inner work first. I think it was only my tenacity and willingness to grit my teeth and get on with it that enabled me to actually graduate. As a consequence of that experience, I subconsciously believed I couldn't trust female leaders.

Despite the sadness I feel when I think of what our relationship could have been, I'm unbelievably grateful to her. She taught me how to keep moving even when people try to hold you down. And she also taught me how not to act in the role of mentor. Back then, I wanted a mentor who was supportive, loving, kind, honest, gave me permission, showed me my truth and looked for the hidden treasure within me. This is what I do with all of my clients and it's a potent recipe for growth and liberation.

I believe deep down, we all want to sink into the loving embrace of a woman who's rooting for us. It feels good to allow ourselves to be seen, heard and understood. It feels radical to allow ourselves to be held. There's nothing quite like it for our sense of wellbeing and connection.

LIVING YOUR PRIESTESSHOOD

Following our callings and channelling them into something tangible like a business or a project is a potent way to embody or externalise our priestesshood, and it's certainly been an incredible vehicle for self-actualisation for me. Yet priestesshood goes far beyond that. It's a way of being. It's not what we do. It's not what we create. It's who we are. The priestess is the energy that brings about healing, truth, justice and expansion. When we let that in, in all areas of our lives, we naturally embody her energy.

Priestesshood is about embracing the alchemic nature of all experiences and using life as our fuel for growth. It's not about being pious or virtuous. It's not about running back to safety. It's not about waiting to feel ready before we act. It's about running into the fire to reclaim our wild essence, our feminine experience, and our almost frightening desire to touch the world deeply and change the world drastically.

There are days when we must let ourselves be messy, chaotic and less than eloquent. The part of us that rejects this wildness, this humanness, this feminine power, is the same part that rejects imperfection and disorder. And yet also the same part that craves it.

We crave freedom. For ourselves and for everyone. And the priestess is our portal to it. She demands fierceness, gentleness, compassion, devotion, commitment, love, shadow and light. She wants us to work with them all.

You're here for a reason. There is magic within you, and after reading this book, you now understand that the beliefs you have about not being good enough or worthy enough, are illusions. Those internal stories are hallmarks of the internalised oppression that have been etched into your being since you were born. But now that you know this, the illusion has been shattered. What you do now is up to you.

The only way to create the clarity and confidence to live life on your terms and live your priestesshood is to lean into your fears and recognise that, on the other side of fear, there's expansion and growth. Confidence and clarity are the results of simply taking one step and then another. As you follow your highest excitement, the next steps will then be made known to you. This is priestesshood.

ILLUMINATE & TRANSCEND
End of Chapter Contemplations

Contemplation is the process of bringing something into our awareness and allowing the light of our consciousness to reveal the layers of its meaning to us time and time again. It encourages true transformation by providing space for us to gain deeper clarity on our insights and integrate them into our lives.

You can contemplate through journalling or by going for a walk in nature and asking yourself the question over and over again.

Don't rush through this process. Give yourself space and time for the wisdom to emerge and you'll be blown away by what you discover.

Here are the contemplative prompts for this chapter:

- *Feel back into the woman you were before reading this book — who was she?*

- *Who have you now become?*

- *What have been your biggest breakthroughs throughout?*

- *Moving forward, what will you commit to on your journey to priestesshood?*

EPILOGUE

I'm sat here writing these concluding thoughts on the veranda of my Portuguese house that overlooks the ocean. The sun is still strong on my skin. It's a quiet Saturday and all I can hear is birdsong and the occasional contented sigh coming from my dog who's lying loyally at my feet. Mauro is in the kitchen cooking something delicious and I feel so at peace.

Here in the Algarve, we live simple lives. My day usually consists of cuddles and deep talks with Mauro, a few hours of work (which never feels like work because I love it so much), long dog walks, tending to our growing vegetables, and sunset catch-ups with friends and wine. All in all, we're here for simplicity and sustainable abundance. It's not always idyllic of course. Mauro and I sometimes have fights, the kind that make you question everything. My family (whom I love deeply by the way) still trigger me to act like a teenager from time to time. And every time I up-level in my life, I experience fear and anxiety. And yet I'm more content and fulfilled than ever before. Six years ago, I didn't believe that this could ever be my reality. Why? Because I didn't see my worth. I didn't know what I was capable of. And I didn't understand that all I needed to do to make a difference and cultivate freedom was to follow the callings of the priestess and get comfortable with being uncomfortable.

As I'm sat here, reflecting upon my journey so far, I'm wondering what words to leave you with. What do I wish I'd heard all those years ago?

I think it can be summed up in three words:

Just do it.

Whether it's starting a business, setting up a non-profit, writing a book, creating an album, or growing a herb garden, you're here as a channel. You're here to bring life to the desires inside of you. And you have everything inside of you that you need to make it happen.

Here's the thing, though. You will fail. You will stumble. People will judge you. You will have moments where you doubt yourself so strongly, you almost convince yourself to give up. But you are more qualified and ready then you know. Get started. Now. Not in a month's time. Not when you feel more ready. Dive in now. And then keep going. Remember who you are. You are a daughter of the Divine, a priestess, here to create alchemy and be the vessel through which change happens. We do not live our dharma by waiting. We live it by jumping in fully and committing to continuing to learn the lessons we need to learn and healing the trauma that needs to be healed.

The road to self-actualisation can feel lonely. Surround yourself with people who make you feel sparkly and like you can do anything. Ignore advice from anyone not living the kind of life you want to live. Be bold. Seek teachers and mentors who are rooting for you. Be discerning about the information you consume. Consult with your inner priestess often. And know that whenever you follow any idea that makes you feel excited and expansive, you're on the right path.

I believe in you.

ACKNOWLEDGMENTS

This book would never have come into being if it weren't for the leading man in my life, my partner in crime and soon-to-be husband. Mauro, I'm deeply grateful for your endless support and curiosity. Our long forest walks with Manny, where we heart-riff about life and the universe, sustain and inspire me. You're the life partner I never dared to hope for. Thank you for all that you are, all that you do, and all that you're becoming.

Thank you to my family for finally giving up on the idea of me having an academic career and instead choosing to support me as I navigated my own unique way of being in the world. I know I gave you lots of sleepless nights but we eventually learned that all we needed to do was to trust my process.

Thank you to all of my friends, clients, students, and mentors. In honest communication and in sisterhood, we have found incredible medicine. We will heal this planet.

And finally, thank you to everyone at The Unbound Press, but in particular Nicola. Your encouragement and excitement for this book spurred me on to commit to it. Thank you for your wisdom and support.

ABOUT THE AUTHOR

An archaeologist turned women's mentor, Sarah Coxon, PhD, is a modern-day priestess. Her writing and mentoring programmes help women reclaim their feminine power and divine purpose.

You can find out more about her work and get access to free resources at **www.drsarahcoxon.com**

CPSIA information can be obtained
at www.ICGtesting.com
Printed in the USA
BVHW041043050121
597035BV00010B/559